Proclai

The Name of God Book

Proclaiming God's Word

The Name of God Book

108
Scriptures
About God's
Sovereign Name

Diana Scimone
peapod publishing inc.

The Name of God Book
© 2017 by Diana Scimone
All rights reserved
Peapod Publishing, Inc., Lake Mary, Florida U.S.A.

ISBN 978-1-63360-902-0
Printed in the United States of America
Cover by Valerie Kosky
www.peapodpublishing.com

This book or parts thereof may not be reproduced in any form, stored in a retrieval system or transmitted in any form by any means—electronic, mechanical, photocopy, recording or otherwise—without prior written permission of the publisher, except as provided by United States of America copyright law.
For translation rights, please contact the publisher.

Scriptures marked AMP taken from the Amplified® Bible, Copyright © 1954, 1958, 1962, 1964, 1965, 1987 by The Lockman Foundation. Used by permission. (www.Lockman.org). Scriptures marked KJV taken from the King James Version. Scripture quotations marked TLB: From The Living Bible, copyright ©1971. Used by permission of Tyndale House Publishers, Inc., Wheaton, IL 60189 USA. All rights reserved. Scriptures marked MEV taken from The Holy Bible, Modern English Version. Copyright © 2014 by Military Bible Association. Published and distributed by Charisma House. All rights reserved. Scriptures marked NAS taken from the New American Standard Bible®, Copyright © 1960, 1962, 1963, 1968, 1971, 1972, 1973, 1975, 1977, 1995 by The Lockman Foundation. Used by permission. (www.Lockman.org). Scriptures marked NIV taken from the HOLY BIBLE, NEW INTERNATIONAL VERSION®. NIV®. Copyright ©1973, 1978, 1984 by International Bible Society. All rights reserved. Scriptures marked NKJ taken from the New King James Version. Copyright © 1982 by Thomas Nelson, Inc. Used by permission. Inc., Carol Stream, Illinois 60188. All rights reserved. All rights reserved.

"The name that is above every name" (Philippians 2:9 NIV)

In just about every culture in the world, naming a baby is important. In many African countries, for example, babies are named at an elaborate ceremony. Jewish parents give their child a contemporary name as well as a Hebrew name, which often has significance to the family.

In many cultures, naming a new baby is an honor reserved for grandparents or other family elders. I'm not a family elder, but I was present when a name was chosen for one of my nephews, and it was a great honor I'll remember forever.

Names are important and they can be powerful—but there is one name that is above all names. In fact, the Bible tells us that every knee will bow before His name (see Philippians 2:9-10). What other name is a strong tower that we can run into (see Proverbs 18:10), allows us to overcome our enemies (see Psalm 44:5), is more powerful than swords and spears (see 1 Samuel 17:45), pulls us from the lowest pit of despair (see Lamentations 3:55), and frees us from death (see Psalm 116:3-4)?

What other name endures forever (see Psalm 135:13) and will be remembered throughout all generations (see Psalm 45:17)?

Only one name has all this power and honor: the name above all names. The early believers knew the sovereignty of that name, which is one of the reasons the church expanded rapidly throughout the world. In fact, almost 20% of the Scripture verses in this book are from the book of Acts—because calling on the power of God's name and decreeing, declaring, and proclaiming it was critical to the expansion of God's Kingdom.

Even God's enemies know the power of His name, which is why they try to silence any mention of it: "They...commanded them not to speak or teach at all in the name of Jesus. But Peter and John answered them, 'Whether it is right in the sight of God to listen to you more than to God, you judge. For we cannot help but declare what we have seen and heard'" (Acts 4:18-20 NAS).

May we also recognize the power of His name and boldly declare it and proclaim it in our communities and across the world.

☐ ☐ ☐

> Don't miss *The Titles of God Book* with more than 100 scriptures about God's captivating character and His many titles such as the Rock, Lamb of God, Desire of All Nations, King of the Nations, and more.

How to use this book

The Name of God Book has more than 100 scriptures about God's sovereign name—for you, for your neighbors, your city, and your country.

Read each verse out loud as a powerful decree. This is what you are actually doing: "You will also decree a thing, and it will be established for you" (Job 22:28 NAS). You decree; God establishes it for you. That's a fantastic partnership, isn't it?

After you read the verses out loud, you can also pray your own prayer of declaration and decree based on the verses. There are two sample prayers later in this section.

As you proclaim God's Word out loud, remember four things:

1. The power of Hebrews 4:12: "The word of God is living and powerful, and sharper than any

two-edged sword, piercing even to the division of soul and spirit, and of joints and marrow, and is a discerner of the thoughts and intents of the heart" (NKJ). That's what happens when you read the Word out loud and proclaim it over your city.

2. The power of Ephesians 2:6: "God raised us up with Christ and seated us with him in the heavenly realms in Christ Jesus" (NIV). Did you notice this verse is in the past tense—seated? You have already been seated with Him in heavenly places. You don't have to wait until eternity for that privilege. And you're there not just to sit, but to rule and reign with Him now. That's reality! That means if the unjust can "issue oppressive decrees" (Isaiah 10:1 NIV), you can issue righteous ones.

3. The power of Romans 8:11: "The Spirit of Him who raised Jesus from the dead dwells in you" (NKJ). As a born-again believer in Jesus, your authority over strongholds is because of who is living inside you. The enemy knows the power you have

access to and that's why he tries so hard to silence you. Don't let him!

4. Effective, strategic prayer doesn't require yelling at God or begging Him to do something; He already wants things to change and invites you to partner with Him to make that happen. Just as paradigm shifting, there's no need to yell at the devil. The volume of your voice really doesn't move him an inch—but proclaiming God's Word in areas where the enemy has a stronghold? Watch out! Things are about to change!

You're about to go on a great adventure with God declaring His sovereign name across the globe—and across the street.

Where you can proclaim God's Word aloud or silently

- In your home
- Churches, synagogues, mosques
- Walking around your neighborhood
- Waiting at traffic lights or on the drive-through line at the bank or coffee shop
- Schools: elementary, middle, high
- Colleges, universities, trade schools, other institutions of learning
- Playgrounds and parks
- Office or workplace on breaks
- Government offices: local, county, state, federal, international
- Courthouses
- Police stations
- Radio and TV stations, newspapers
- Public transportation stations and systems: subway, bus, trains, airports (and on each of these as you travel)

- Waterways and shipyards
- Power facilities
- Military installations
- Jails and prisons
- Places of entertainment
- Hospitals, nursing homes, medical facilities
- Abortion clinics, strip clubs, massage parlors
- Businesses, stores, factories, malls
- Places of historic significance in your city
- Major interstates
- Via Google maps where you can zoom in to any city around the world and proclaim God's Word over it

Sample prayers
of declaration and decree

Scripture verse #1:

"Your name is like perfume poured out" (Song of Songs 1:3 NIV).

Sample prayer:

Just as a single drop of perfume can permeate an entire room and change the atmosphere—that is what Your name is like. The mere mention of it can overwhelm the stench of sin. It doesn't cover it up; it changes it. It cleanses and replaces it, like beauty for ashes.

So I pour out Your name on those I love who are so blinded by the god of this world. I pour out Your name on them, just like perfume. I stand on my own testimony of how lost I was until You poured out Your name on me—Your love, Your power, Your kindness, Your sweetness, Your very name and all that is in it.

I pour out Your powerful mighty name that shatters strongholds because Your name is Your presence. Your name is Your power. Your name is Your love for us poured out on us. Just as Mary poured out her perfume on Your feet as a sweet, lavish, extravagant, and expensive offering, You pour out Your name on us—sweet, lavish, extravagant, and expensive.

What other name on earth can be mentioned like that? What other name has the power to shatter strongholds, to shatter shame, to change hearts, to melt them, to woo them?

May those I love encounter that name wherever they go. May the fragrance of Your presence follow them like perfume poured out for them. Lavish perfume so expensive that it cost You everything— Your very life.

Scripture verse #2:

"When they had called the apostles, and beaten them, they commanded that they should not speak in the name of Jesus, and let them go. And they departed from the presence of the council, rejoicing that they were counted worthy to suffer shame for his name" (Acts 5:40-41 KJV).

Sample prayer:

Lord, I have to tell You that this verse challenges me. If someone beat me and told me never to speak Your name, would I "count it worthy to suffer shame" for Your name?

It would only be by Your grace that I could do that—by the power of Your name manifest in me to continue proclaiming Your name in the midst of extreme persecution. So many of Your followers live in places where this 2,000-year-old verse is a reality 24/7. They need the power of Your name to continue proclaiming Your name.

So that is what I declare over them—may the same grace that sustained Paul, Silas, and others in the early church be on them. No matter what they encounter, I declare that the power of Your name would sustain them through persecution, betrayal, lies, thefts, beatings, arrests, imprisonment, abandonment, and even death.

I speak the power of Your name over every one of these believers who is being persecuted for Your name's sake. For those in prison. For family members left behind with no means of support. For wives, husbands, children, and parents of those killed for their loyalty to the name above all names.

May You—the name above all names—sustain them in this life and honor them in eternity.

❏ ❏ ❏

The Name of God Book is also available as an ebook so that you can keep these powerful verses on your phone or tablet.

❏ ❏ ❏

"For this purpose I have raised you up, that I may show My power in you, and that My **name** may be declared in all the earth."

—Exodus 9:16 (NKJ)

"I will cause all my goodness to pass in front of you, and I will proclaim my **name**, the Lord, in your presence."

—Exodus 33:19 (NIV)

"And the Lord descended in the cloud, and stood with him there, and proclaimed the **name** of the Lord."
—Exodus 34:5 (KJV)

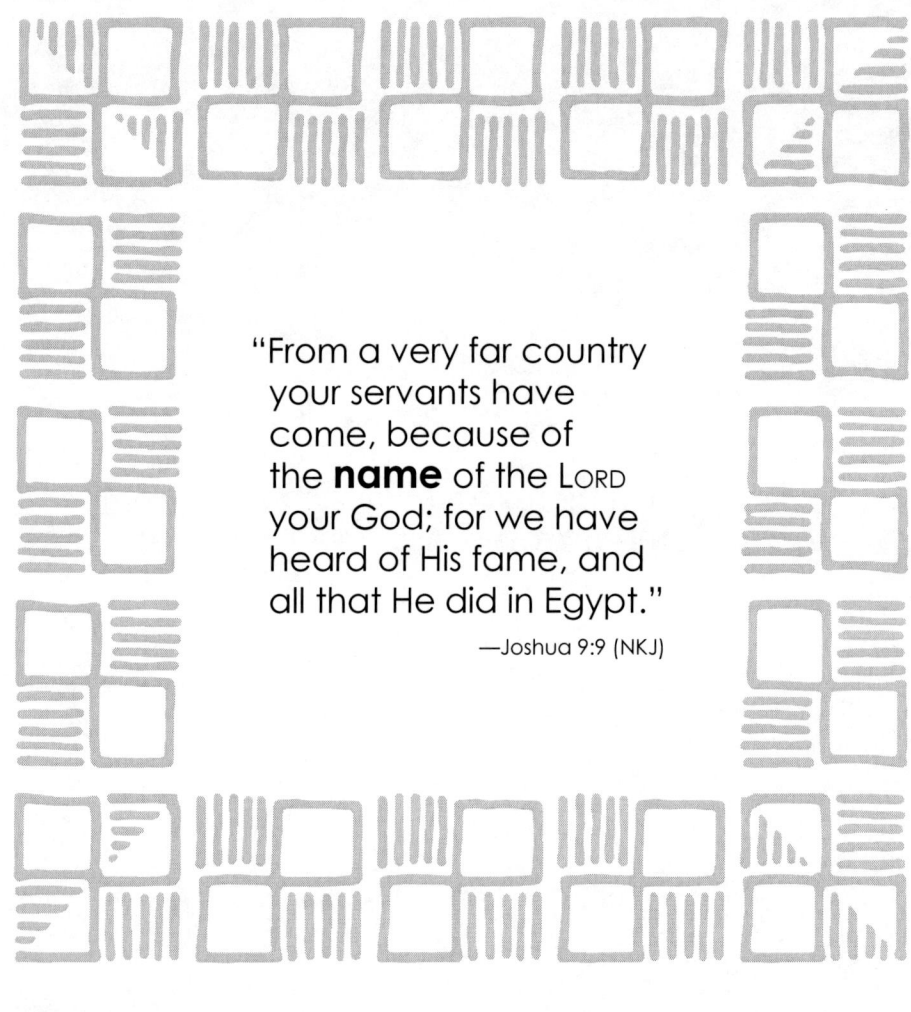

"From a very far country your servants have come, because of the **name** of the Lord your God; for we have heard of His fame, and all that He did in Egypt."

—Joshua 9:9 (NKJ)

"Then David said to the Philistine, 'You come to me with a sword, a spear, and a shield, but I come to you in the **name** of the Lord of Hosts, the God of the armies of Israel, whom you have reviled.'"

—1 Samuel 17:45 (MEV)

"May Your **name** be magnified forever."

—2 Samuel 7:26 (MEV)

"That all peoples of the earth may know Your **name**."

—1 Kings 8:43 (NKJ)

"Now when the queen of Sheba heard about the fame of Solomon concerning the **name** of the LORD, she came to test him with difficult questions."

—1 Kings 10:1 (NAS)

"Then you call on the name of your god, and I will call on the **name** of the Lord, and the God who answers by fire, He is God."

—1 Kings 18:24 (NAS)

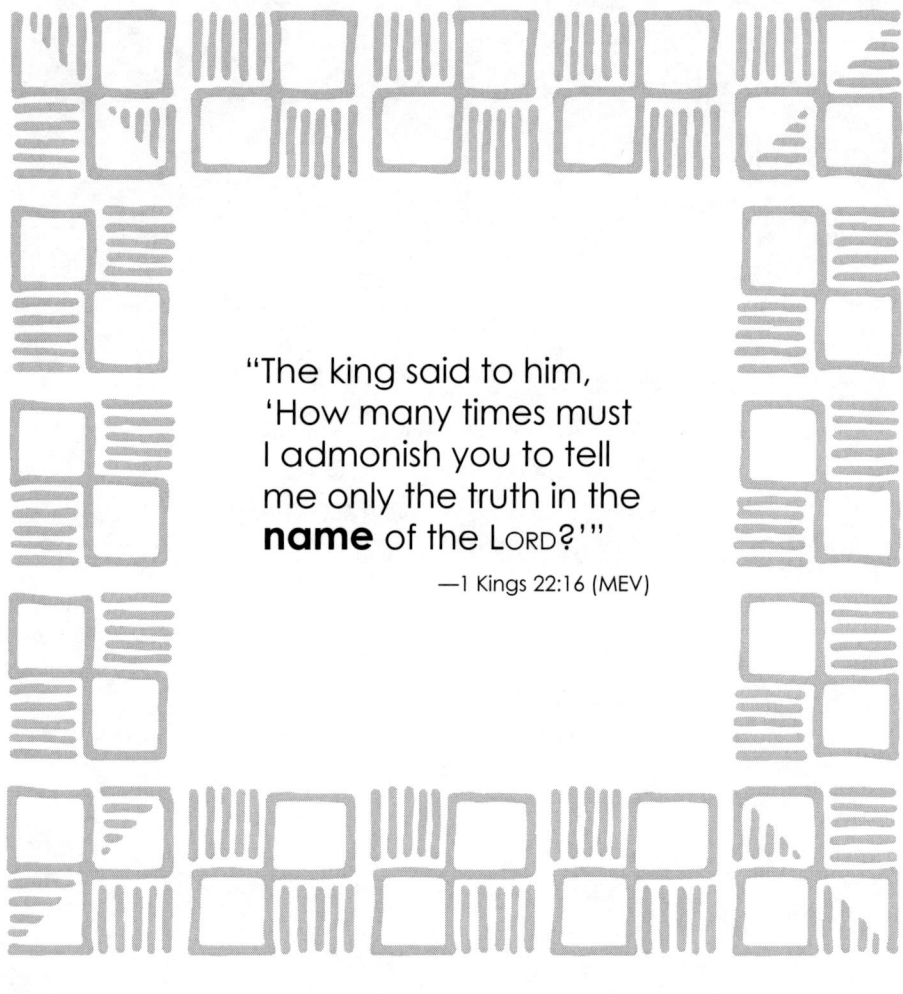

"The king said to him, 'How many times must I admonish you to tell me only the truth in the **name** of the Lord?'"

—1 Kings 22:16 (MEV)

"Give to the Lord the glory due His **name**."

—1 Chronicles 16:29 (NKJ)

"If My people who are called by My **name** will humble themselves, and pray and seek My face, and turn from their wicked ways, then I will hear from heaven, and will forgive their sin and heal their land."

—2 Chronicles 7:14 (NKJ)

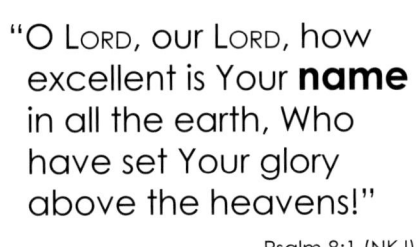

"O Lord, our Lord, how excellent is Your **name** in all the earth, Who have set Your glory above the heavens!"

—Psalm 8:1 (NKJ)

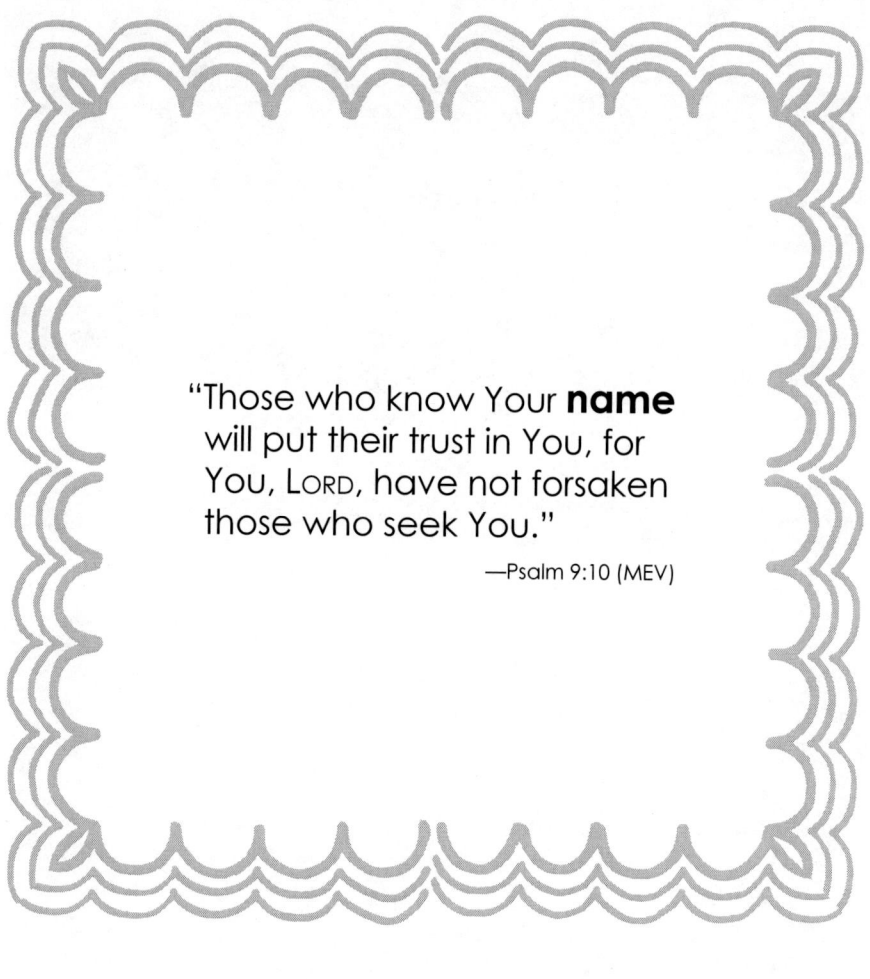

"Those who know Your **name** will put their trust in You, for You, Lord, have not forsaken those who seek You."

—Psalm 9:10 (MEV)

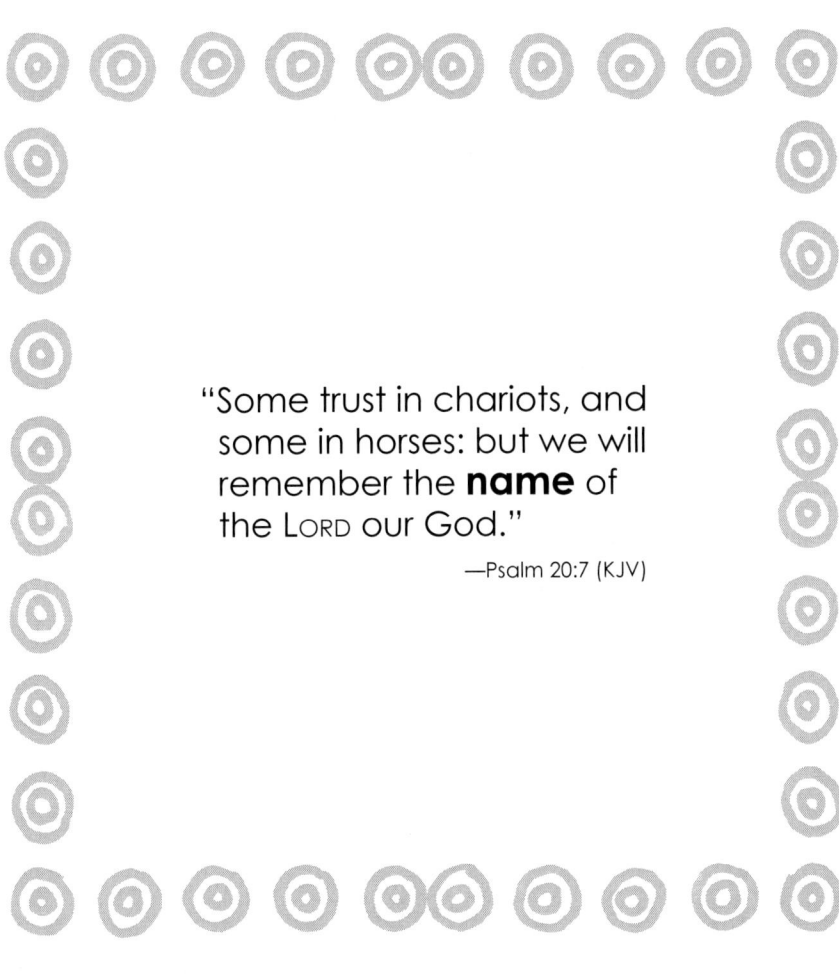

"Some trust in chariots, and some in horses: but we will remember the **name** of the Lord our God."

—Psalm 20:7 (KJV)

"I will declare Your **name** to My brethren."

—Psalm 22:22 (NKJ)

"He restores my soul; He leads me in the paths of righteousness for His **name's** sake."

—Psalm 23:3 (NKJ)

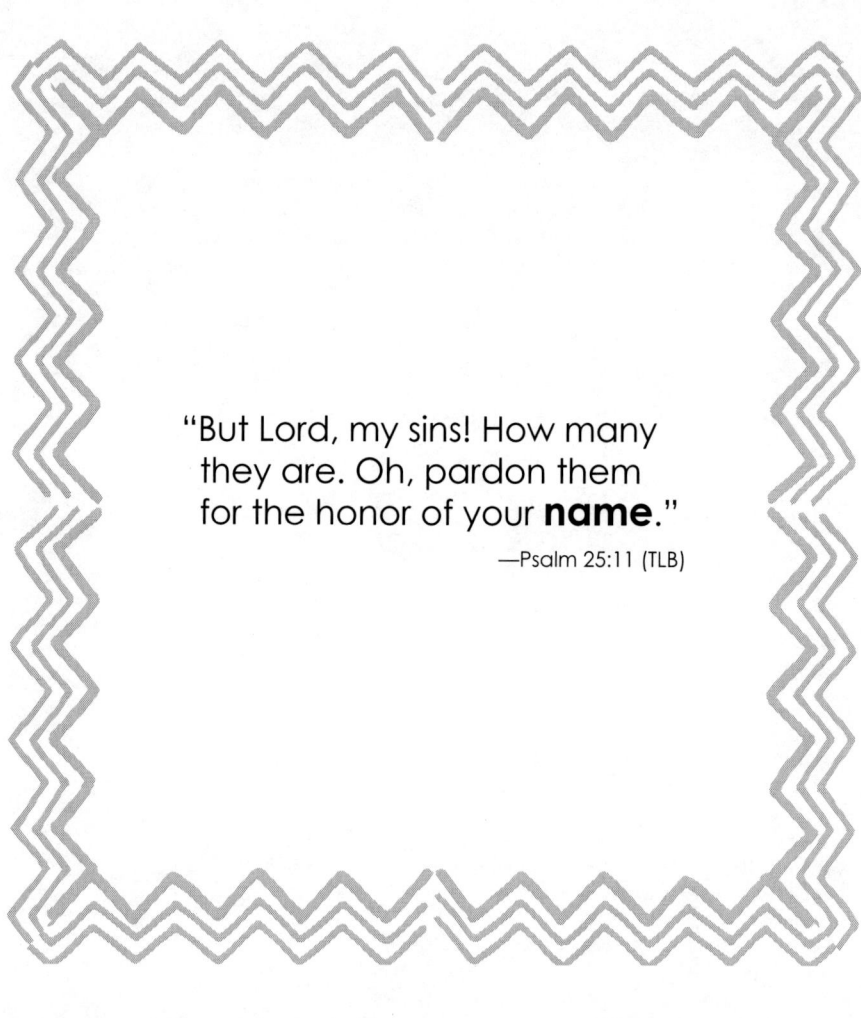

"But Lord, my sins! How many they are. Oh, pardon them for the honor of your **name**."

—Psalm 25:11 (TLB)

"Through You we will push down our opponents; through Your **name** we will trample those who rise up against us."

—Psalm 44:5 (MEV)

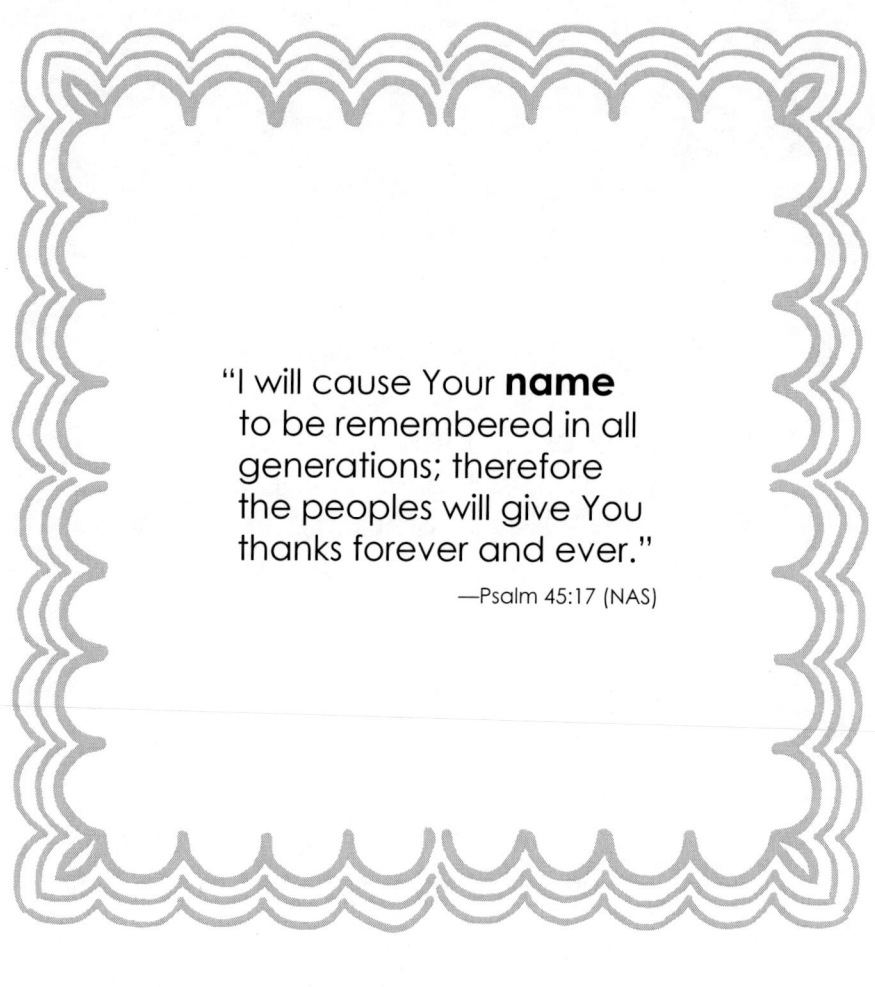

"I will cause Your **name** to be remembered in all generations; therefore the peoples will give You thanks forever and ever."

—Psalm 45:17 (NAS)

"Save me, O God, by thy **name**."

—Psalm 54:1 (KJV)

"You have given me the heritage of those who fear Your **name**."

—Psalm 61:5 (NKJ)

"That men may know that thou, whose **name** alone is Jehovah, art the most high over all the earth."

—Psalm 83:18 (KJV)

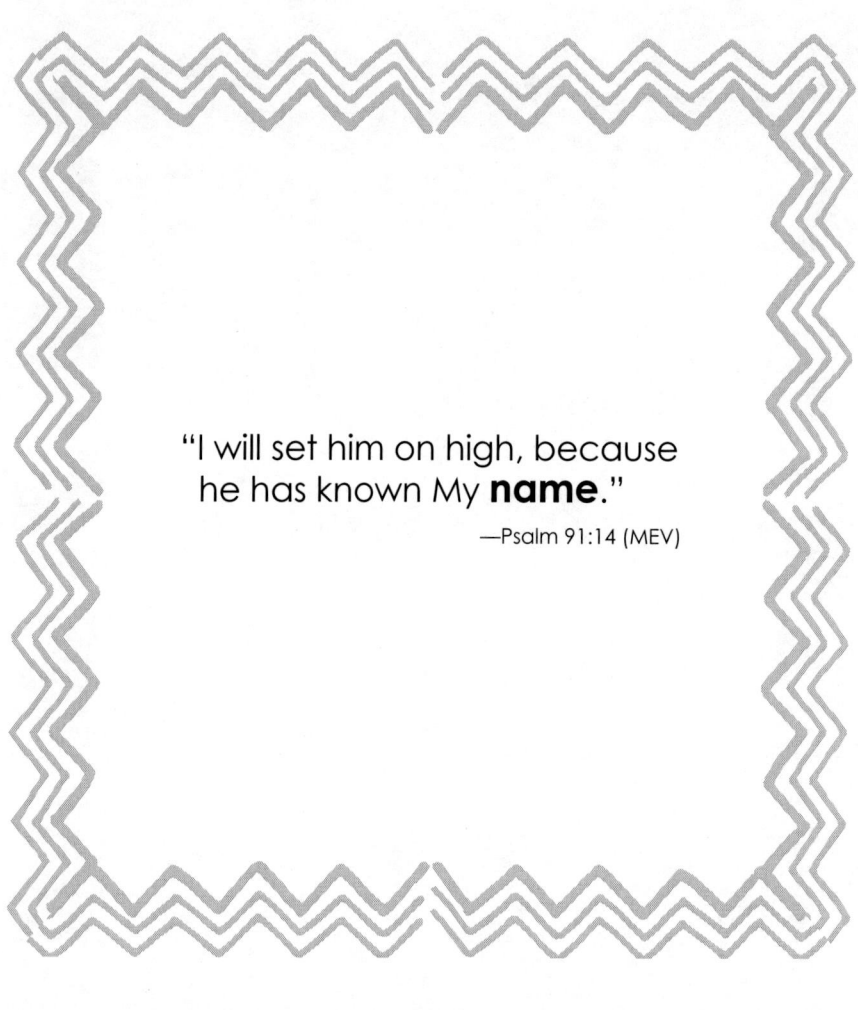

"I will set him on high, because he has known My **name**."

—Psalm 91:14 (MEV)

"So the nations shall fear the **name** of the Lord and all the kings of the earth Your glory."

—Psalm 102:15 (NAS)

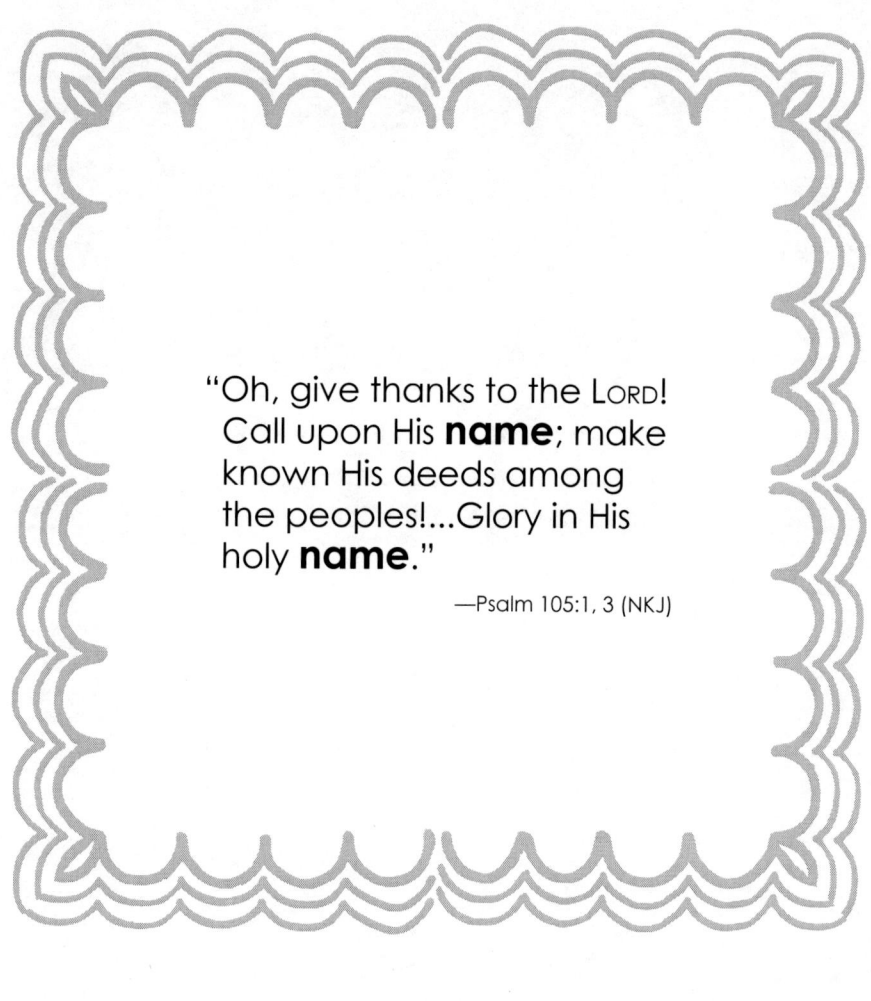

"Oh, give thanks to the LORD! Call upon His **name**; make known His deeds among the peoples!...Glory in His holy **name**."

—Psalm 105:1, 3 (NKJ)

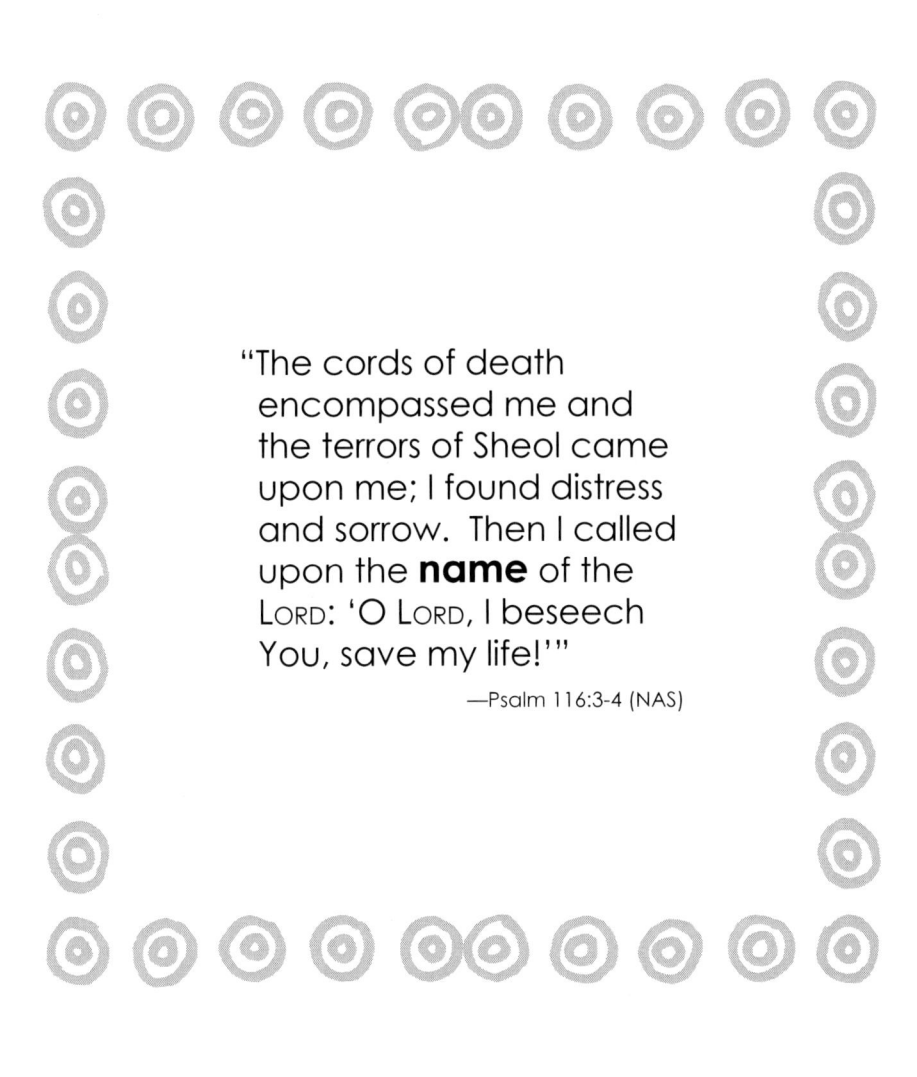

"The cords of death encompassed me and the terrors of Sheol came upon me; I found distress and sorrow. Then I called upon the **name** of the Lord: 'O Lord, I beseech You, save my life!'"

—Psalm 116:3-4 (NAS)

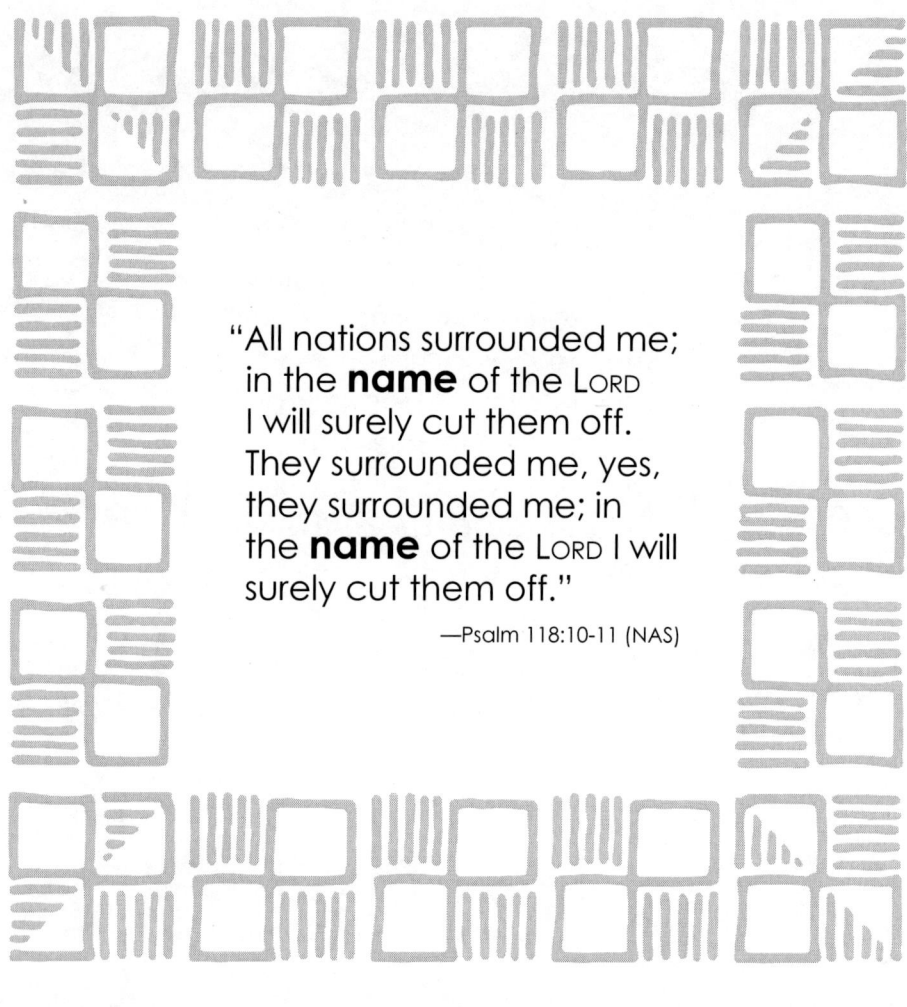

"All nations surrounded me; in the **name** of the Lord I will surely cut them off. They surrounded me, yes, they surrounded me; in the **name** of the Lord I will surely cut them off."

—Psalm 118:10-11 (NAS)

"Jerusalem is built as a city that is compact together, where the tribes go up, the tribes of the Lord, to the Testimony of Israel, to give thanks to the **name** of the Lord."

—Psalm 122:3-4 (NKJ)

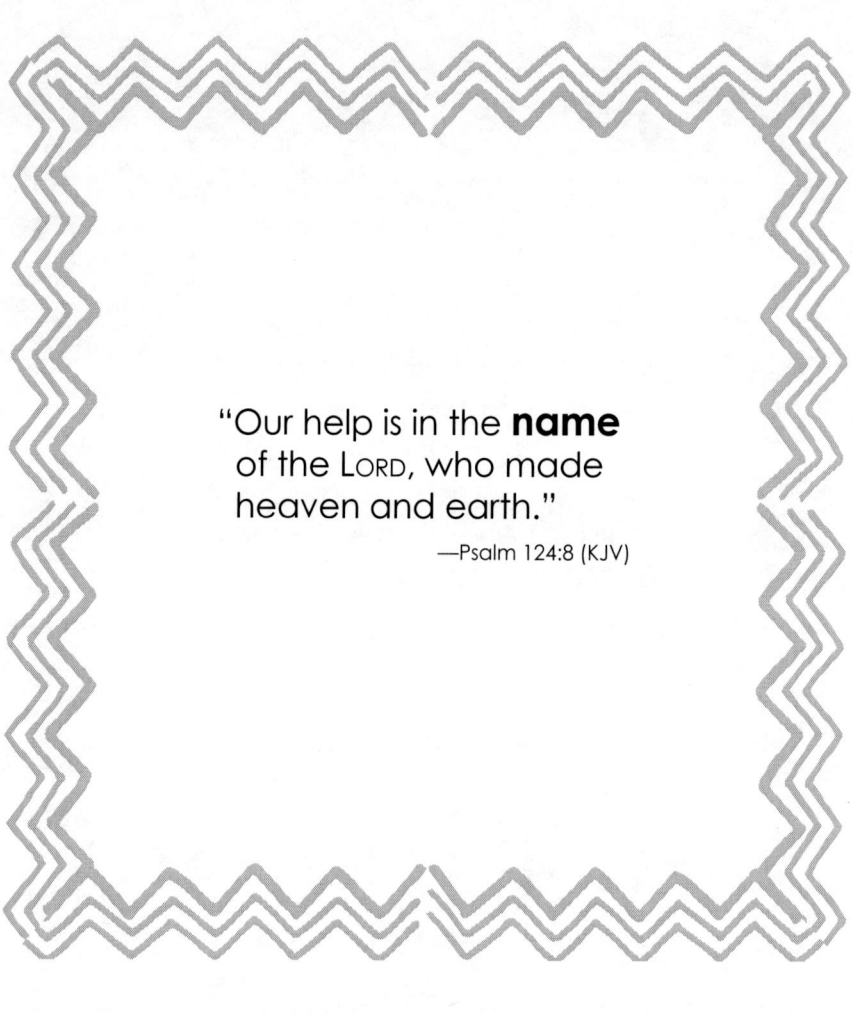

"Our help is in the **name** of the Lord, who made heaven and earth."

—Psalm 124:8 (KJV)

"Thy **name**, O Lord, endureth for ever."

—Psalm 135:13 (KJV)

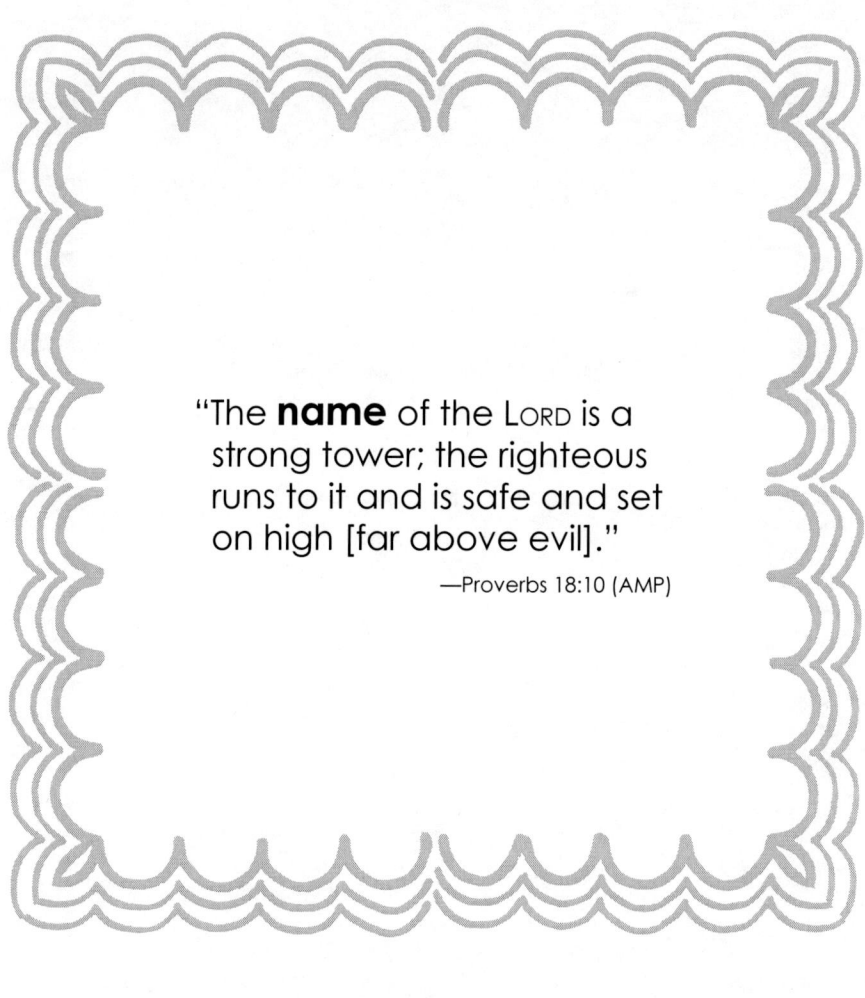

"The **name** of the Lord is a strong tower; the righteous runs to it and is safe and set on high [far above evil]."

—Proverbs 18:10 (AMP)

"Your **name** is like perfume poured out."

—Song of Songs 1:3 (NIV)

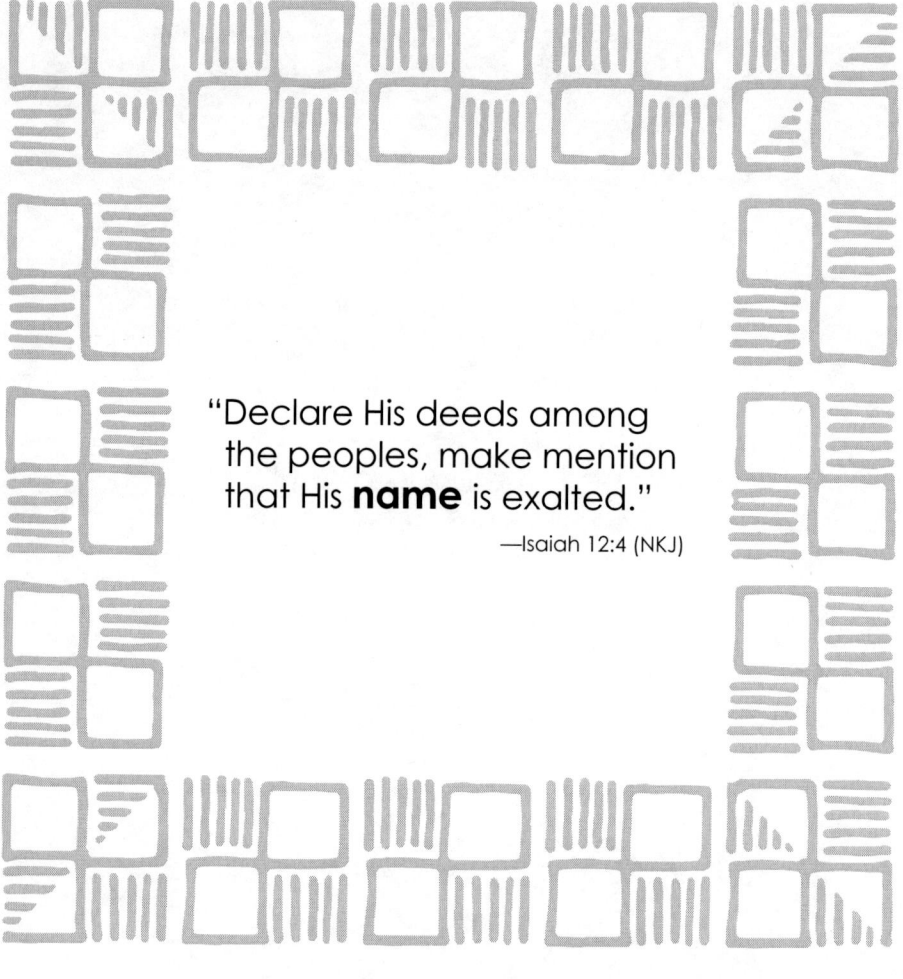

"Declare His deeds among the peoples, make mention that His **name** is exalted."

—Isaiah 12:4 (NKJ)

"The desire of our soul is for Your **name** and for the remembrance of You."

—Isaiah 26:8 (NKJ)

"See, the **name** of the Lord comes from afar, burning with His anger, and its burden is heavy; His lips are full of indignation, and His tongue as a devouring fire."

—Isaiah 30:27 (MEV)

"Every knee in all the world shall bow to me, and every tongue shall swear allegiance to my **name**."

—Isaiah 45:23 (LB)

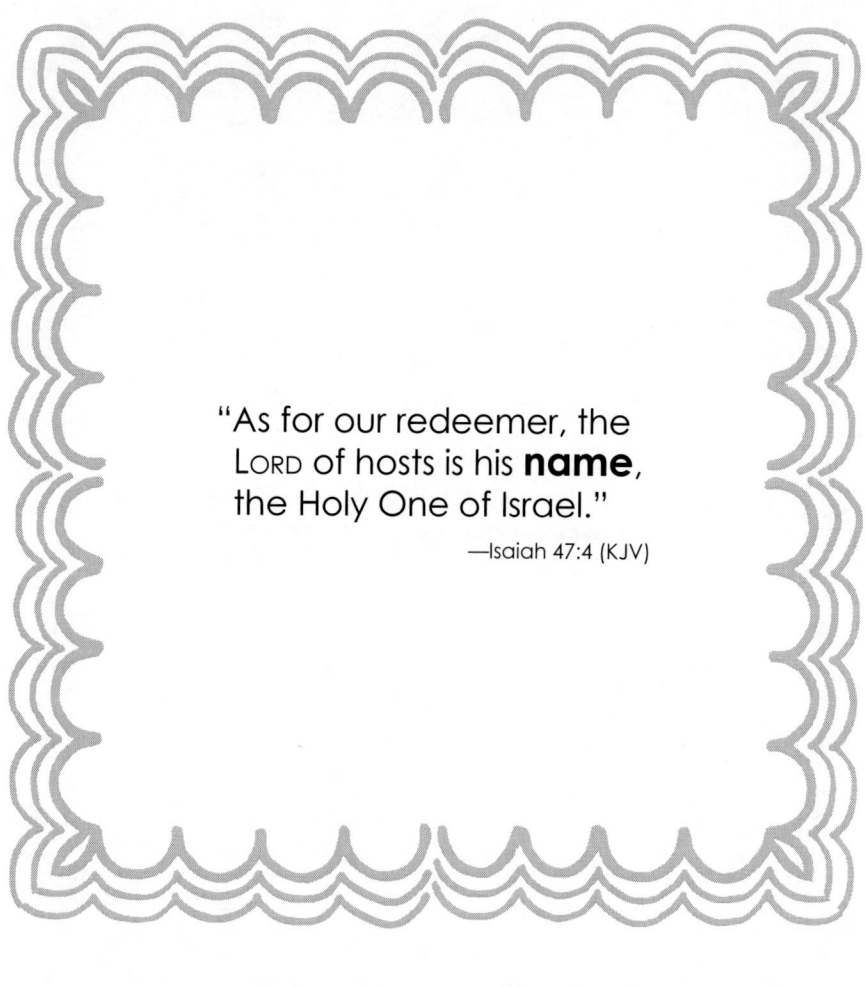

"As for our redeemer, the L͎ᴏʀᴅ of hosts is his **name**, the Holy One of Israel."

—Isaiah 47:4 (KJV)

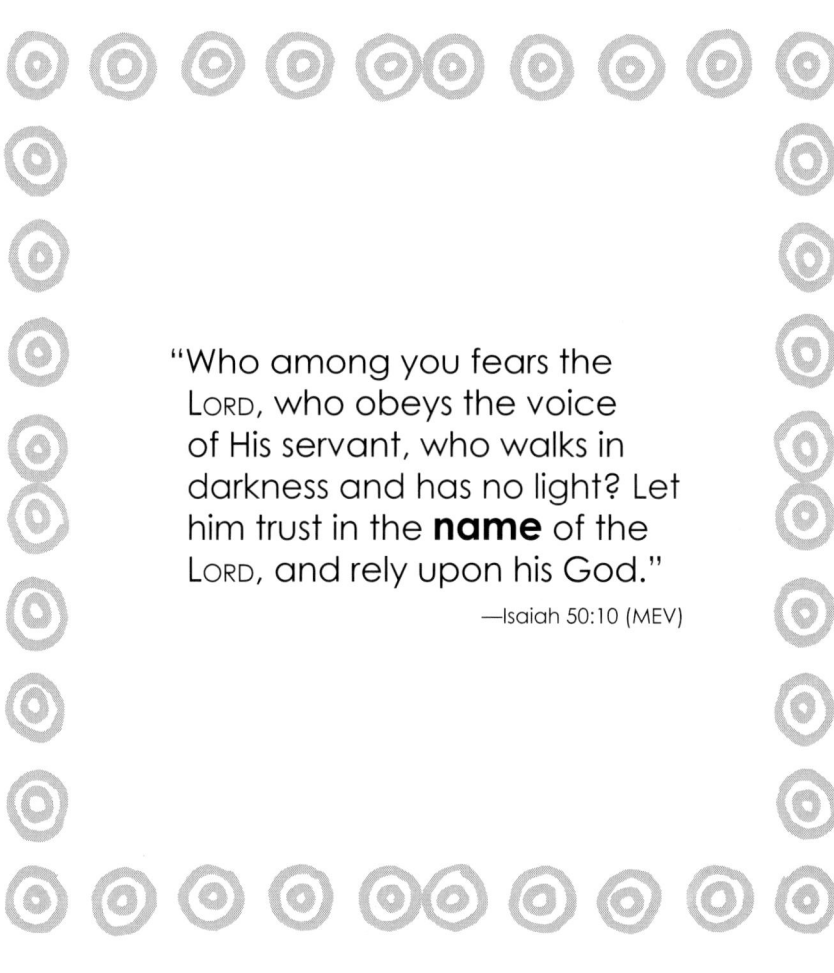

"Who among you fears the Lord, who obeys the voice of His servant, who walks in darkness and has no light? Let him trust in the **name** of the Lord, and rely upon his God."

—Isaiah 50:10 (MEV)

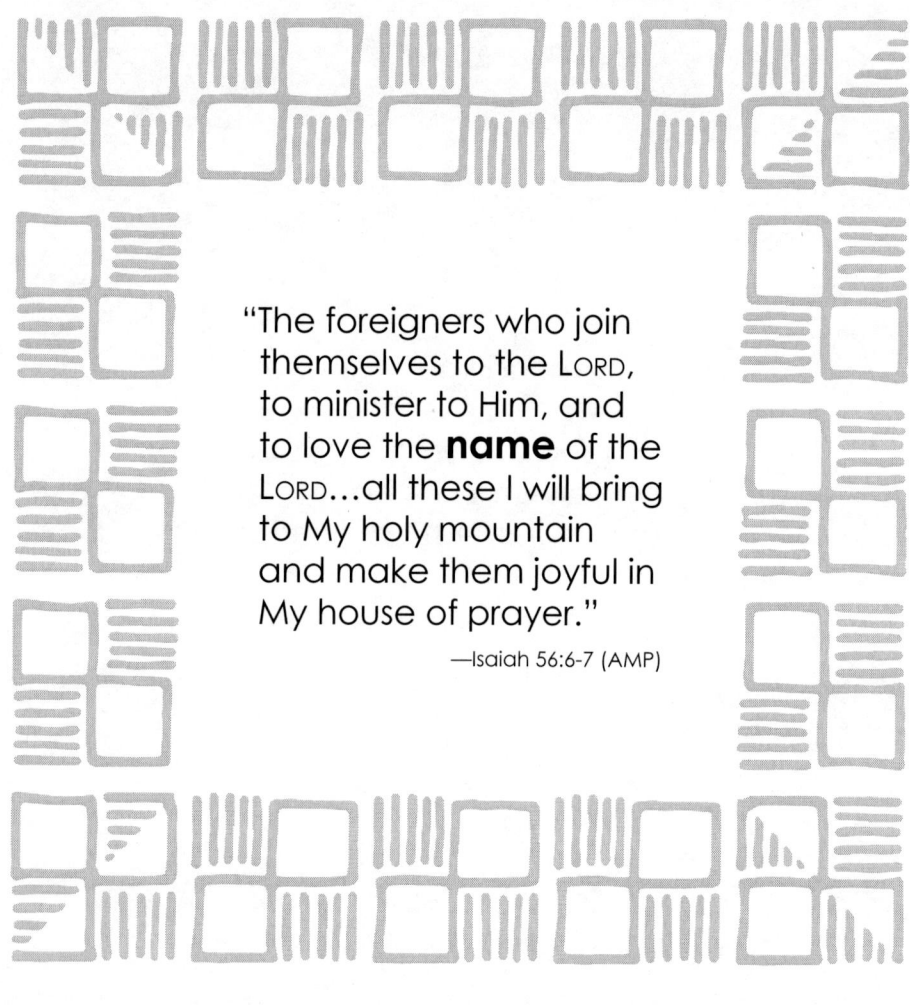

"The foreigners who join themselves to the Lord, to minister to Him, and to love the **name** of the Lord...all these I will bring to My holy mountain and make them joyful in My house of prayer."

—Isaiah 56:6-7 (AMP)

"So shall they fear the **name** of the Lord from the west, and his glory from the rising of the sun."

—Isaiah 59:19 (KJV)

"Surely the coastlands shall wait for Me, and the ships of Tarshish shall come first, to bring your sons from afar, their silver and their gold with them, to the **name** of the Lord your God and to the Holy One of Israel because He has glorified you."

—Isaiah 60:9 (MEV)

"As when fire sets twigs ablaze and causes water to boil, come down to make your **name** known to your enemies and cause the nations to quake before you!"

—Isaiah 64:2 (NIV)

"At that time they shall call Jerusalem the throne of the Lord; and all the nations shall be gathered unto it, to the **name** of the LORD, to Jerusalem."

—Jeremiah 3:17 (KJV)

"For the sake of your **name** do not despise us; do not dishonor your glorious throne. Remember your covenant with us and do not break it."

—Jeremiah 14:21 (NIV)

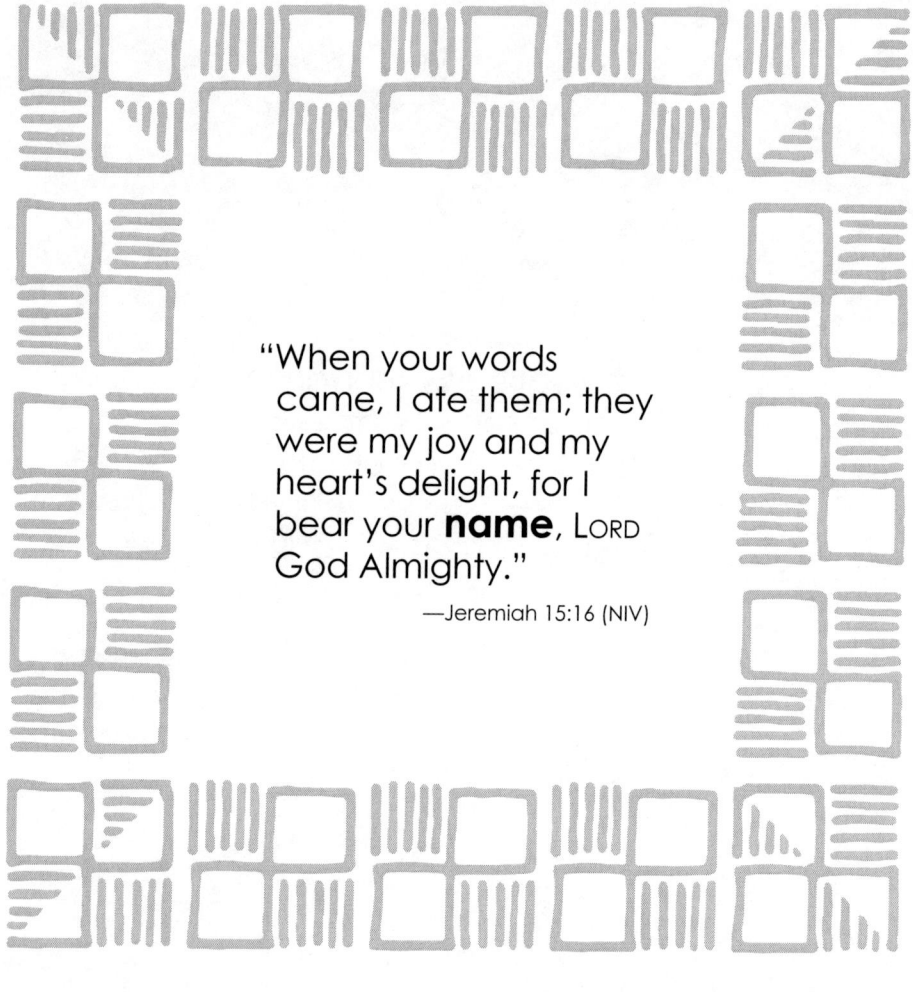

"When your words came, I ate them; they were my joy and my heart's delight, for I bear your **name**, Lord God Almighty."

—Jeremiah 15:16 (NIV)

"I called on Your **name**, O Lord, from the lowest pit."

—Lamentations 3:55 (MEV)

"Everyone who calls on the **name** of the Lord will be saved."

—Joel 2:32 (NIV)

"For all people walk each in the name of his god, but we will walk in the **name** of the Lord our God forever and ever."

—Micah 4:5 (NKJ)

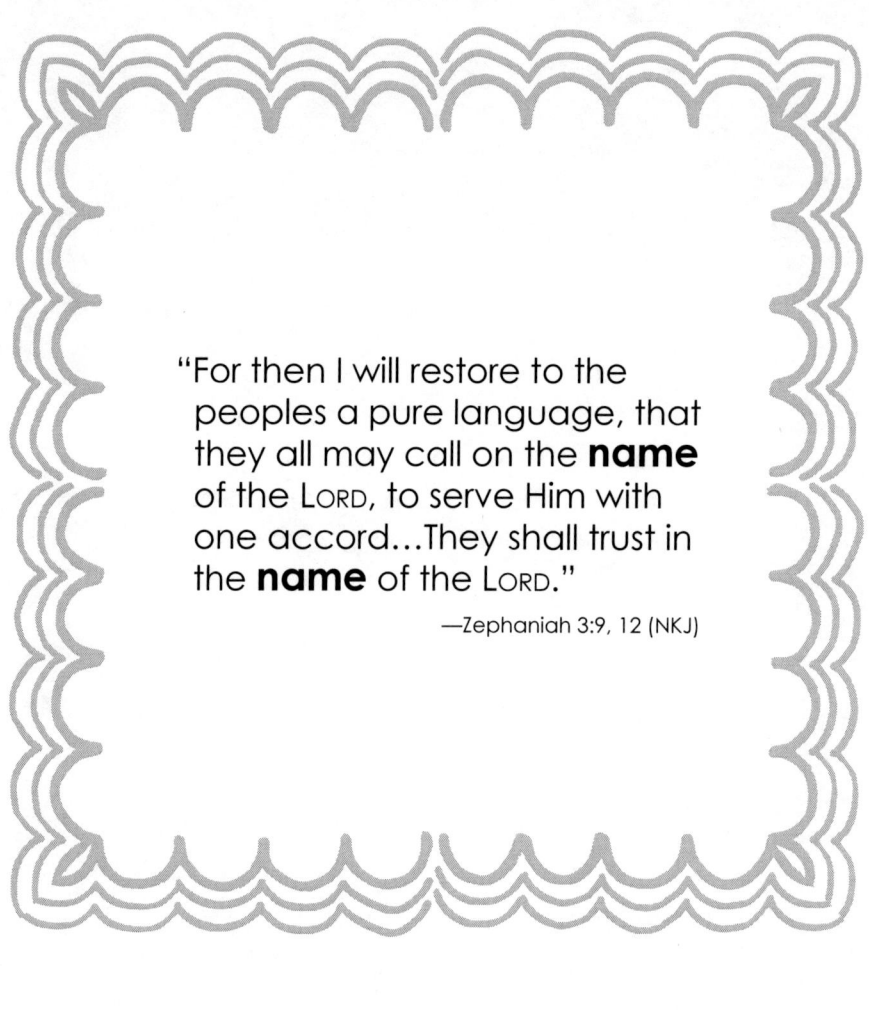

"For then I will restore to the peoples a pure language, that they all may call on the **name** of the Lord, to serve Him with one accord…They shall trust in the **name** of the Lord."

—Zephaniah 3:9, 12 (NKJ)

"I…will refine them as silver is refined, and will try them as gold is tried: they shall call on my **name**, and I will hear them."

—Zechariah 13:9 (KJV)

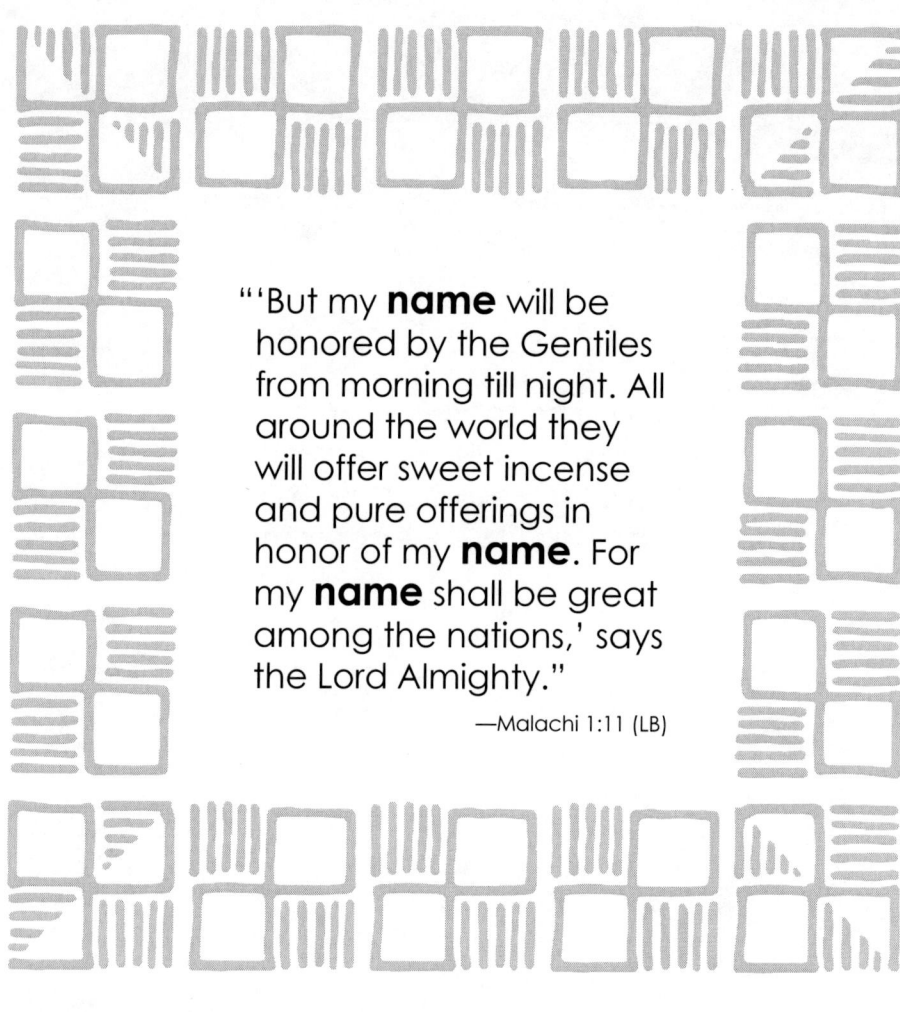

"'But my **name** will be honored by the Gentiles from morning till night. All around the world they will offer sweet incense and pure offerings in honor of my **name**. For my **name** shall be great among the nations,' says the Lord Almighty."

—Malachi 1:11 (LB)

"Then those who feared the Lord spoke to one another, and the Lord gave attention and heard it, and a book of remembrance was written before Him for those who fear the Lord and who esteem His **name**."

—Malachi 3:16 (NAS)

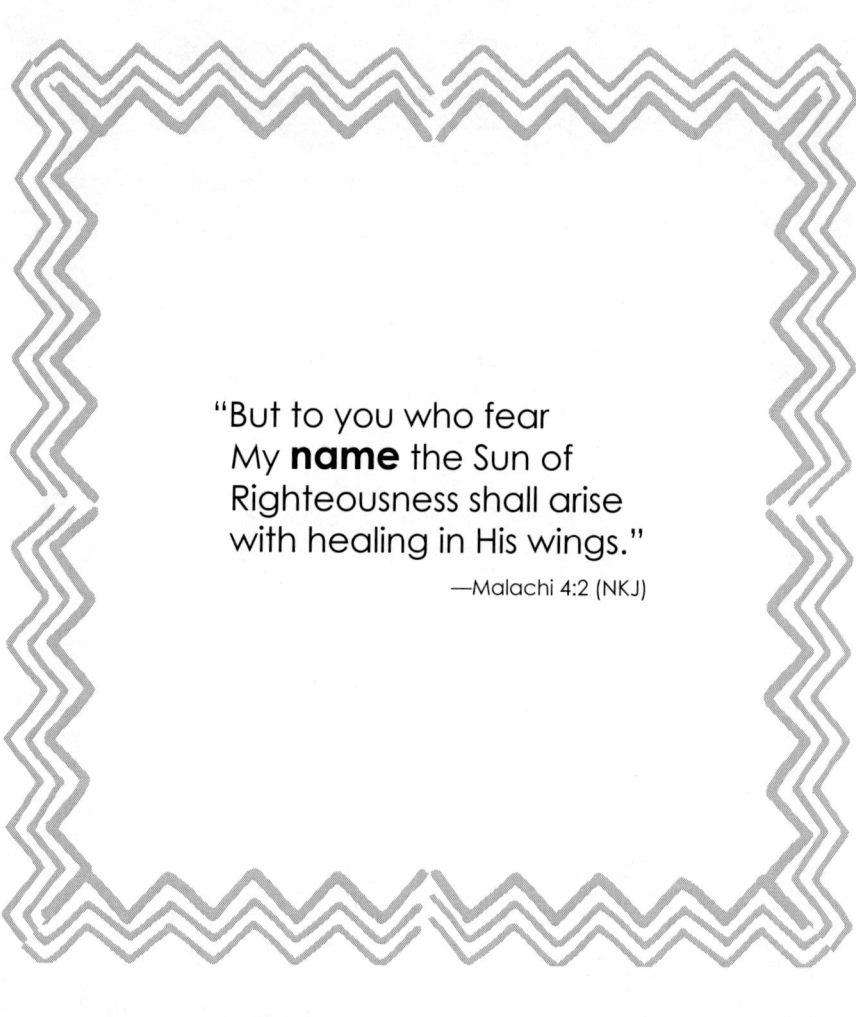

"But to you who fear My **name** the Sun of Righteousness shall arise with healing in His wings."

—Malachi 4:2 (NKJ)

"Many will say to Me in that day, 'Lord, Lord, have we not prophesied in Your **name**, cast out demons in Your **name**, and done many wonders in Your **name**?' And then I will declare to them, 'I never knew you; depart from Me, you who practice lawlessness!'"

—Matthew 7:22-23 (NKJ)

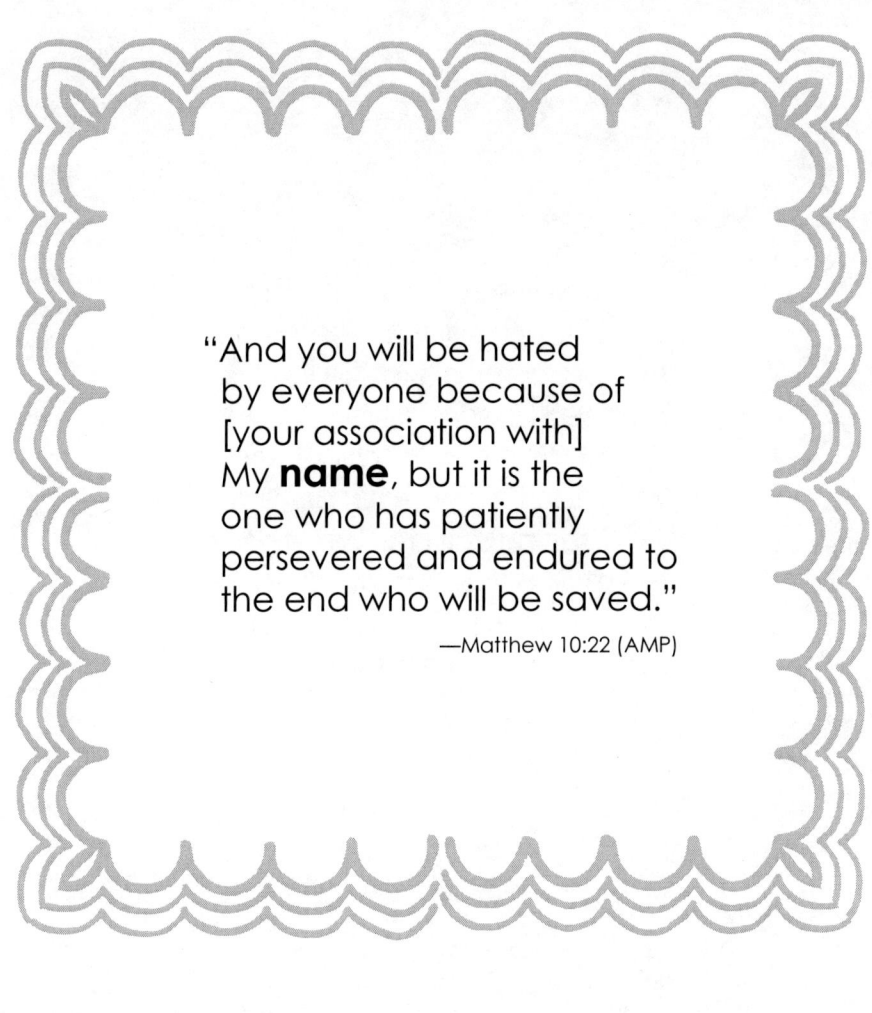

"And you will be hated by everyone because of [your association with] My **name**, but it is the one who has patiently persevered and endured to the end who will be saved."

—Matthew 10:22 (AMP)

"In his **name** the nations will put their hope."

—Matthew 12:21 (NIV)

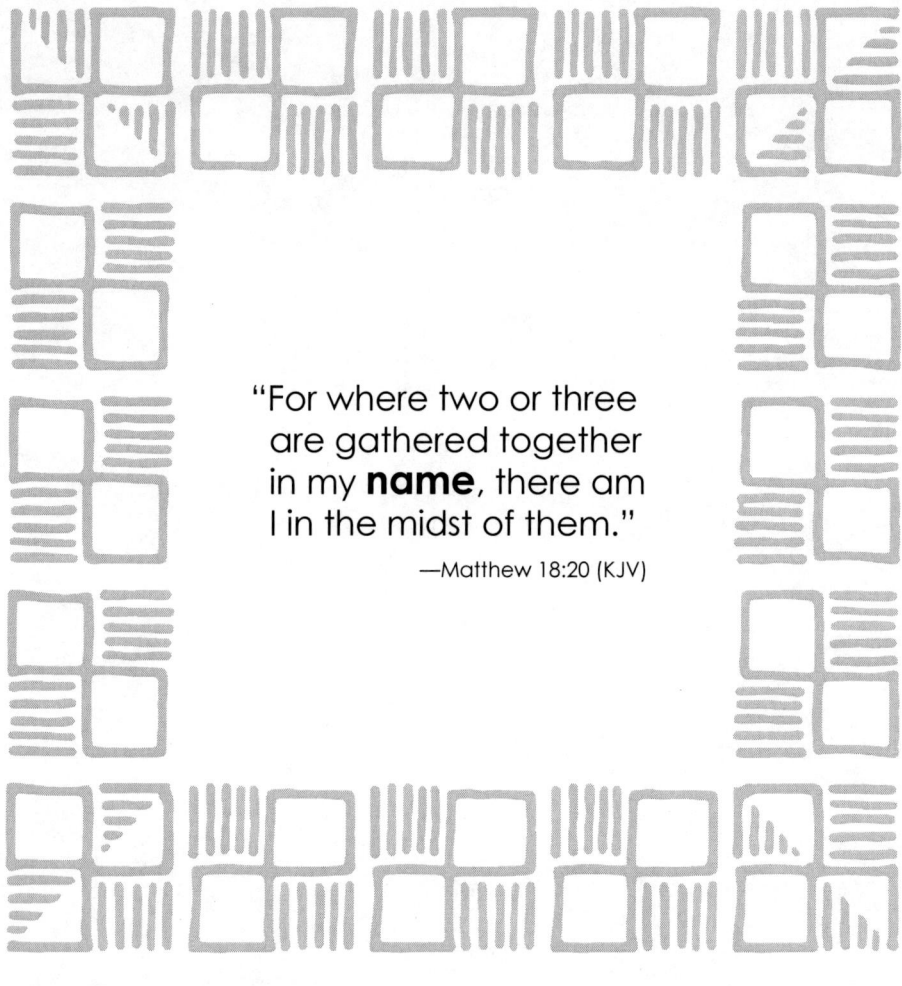

"For where two or three are gathered together in my **name**, there am I in the midst of them."

—Matthew 18:20 (KJV)

"And everyone who has left houses or brothers or sisters or father or mother or wife or children or fields for My **name's** sake shall receive a hundred times as much and inherit eternal life."

—Matthew 19:29 (MEV)

"And the multitudes that went before, and that followed, cried, saying, Hosanna to the son of David: Blessed is he that cometh in the **name** of the Lord; Hosanna in the highest."

—Matthew 21:9 (KJV)

"For I say to you, you shall see Me no more till you say, 'Blessed is He who comes in the **name** of the Lord!'"

—Matthew 23:39 (NKJ)

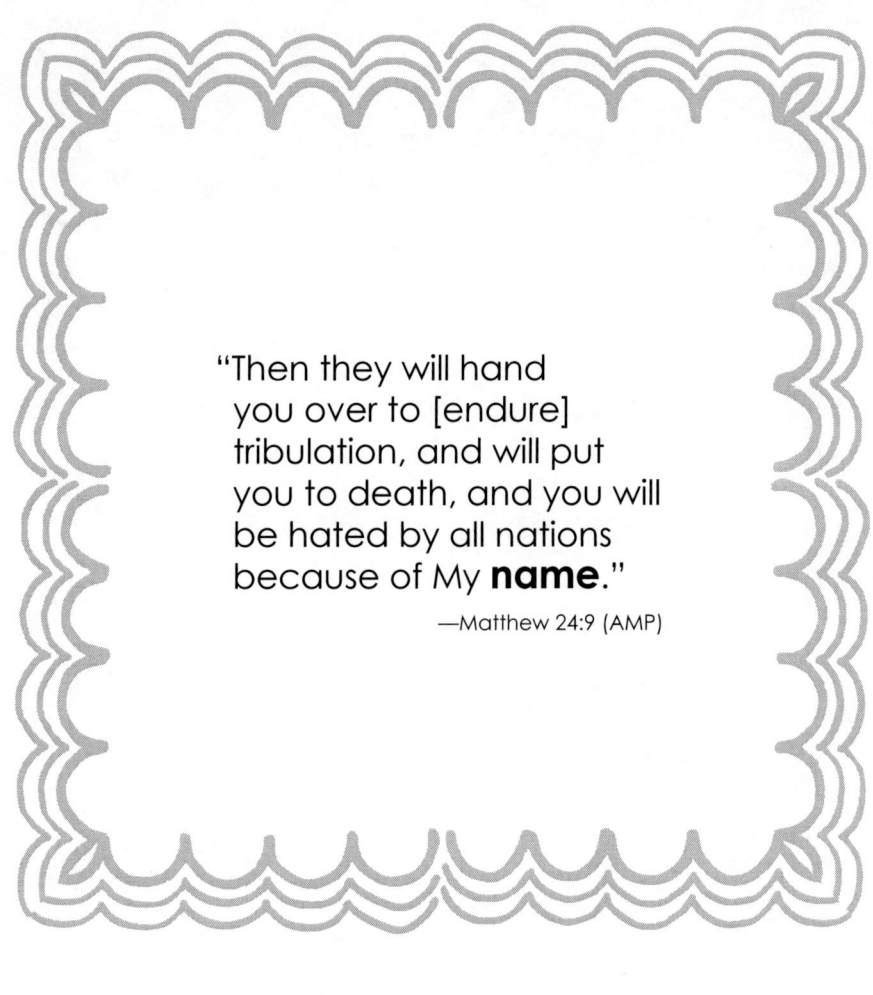

"Then they will hand you over to [endure] tribulation, and will put you to death, and you will be hated by all nations because of My **name**."

—Matthew 24:9 (AMP)

"Whoever receives one of these children in My **name** receives Me. And whoever receives Me receives not Me, but Him who sent Me."

—Mark 9:37 (MEV)

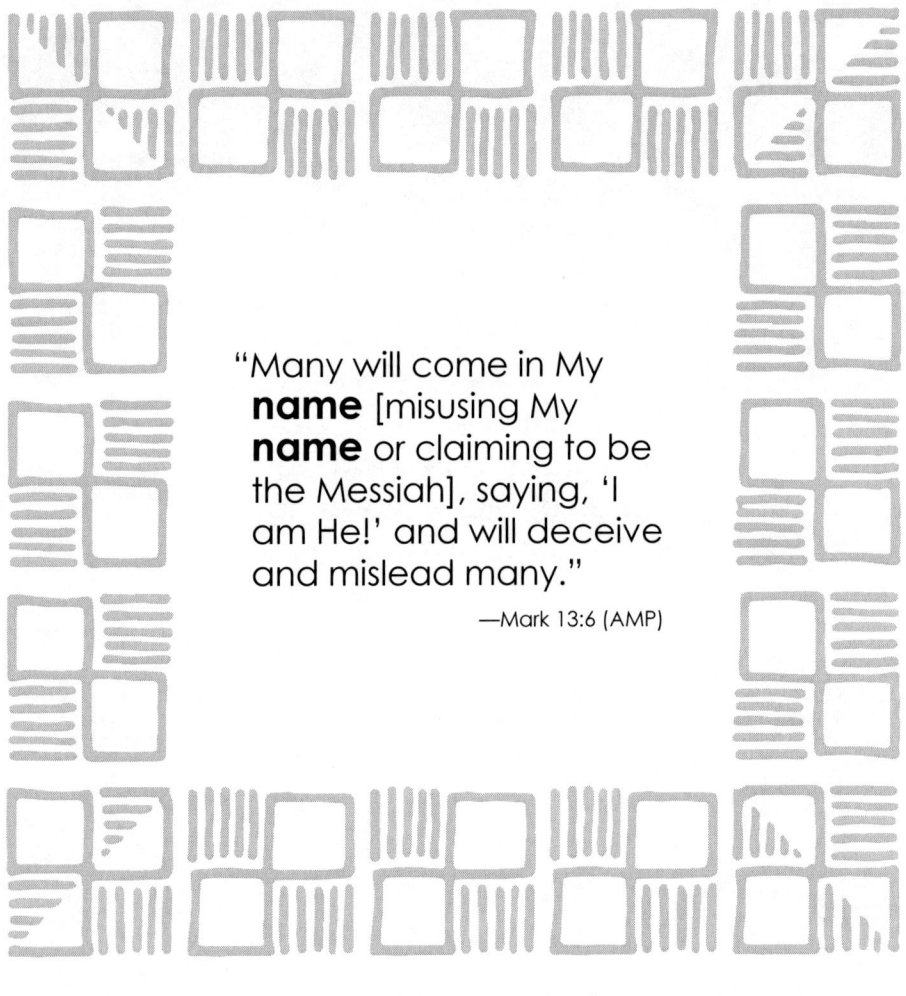

"Many will come in My **name** [misusing My **name** or claiming to be the Messiah], saying, 'I am He!' and will deceive and mislead many."

—Mark 13:6 (AMP)

"You will be hated by everyone because of [your association with] My **name**, but the one who [patiently perseveres empowered by the Holy Spirit and] endures to the end, he will be saved."

—Mark 13:13 (AMP)

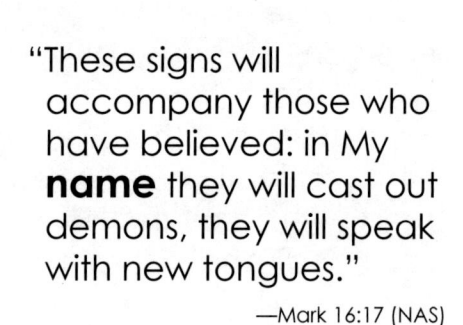

"These signs will accompany those who have believed: in My **name** they will cast out demons, they will speak with new tongues."

—Mark 16:17 (NAS)

"For the Mighty One has done great things for me; and holy is His **name**."

—Luke 1:49 (NAS)

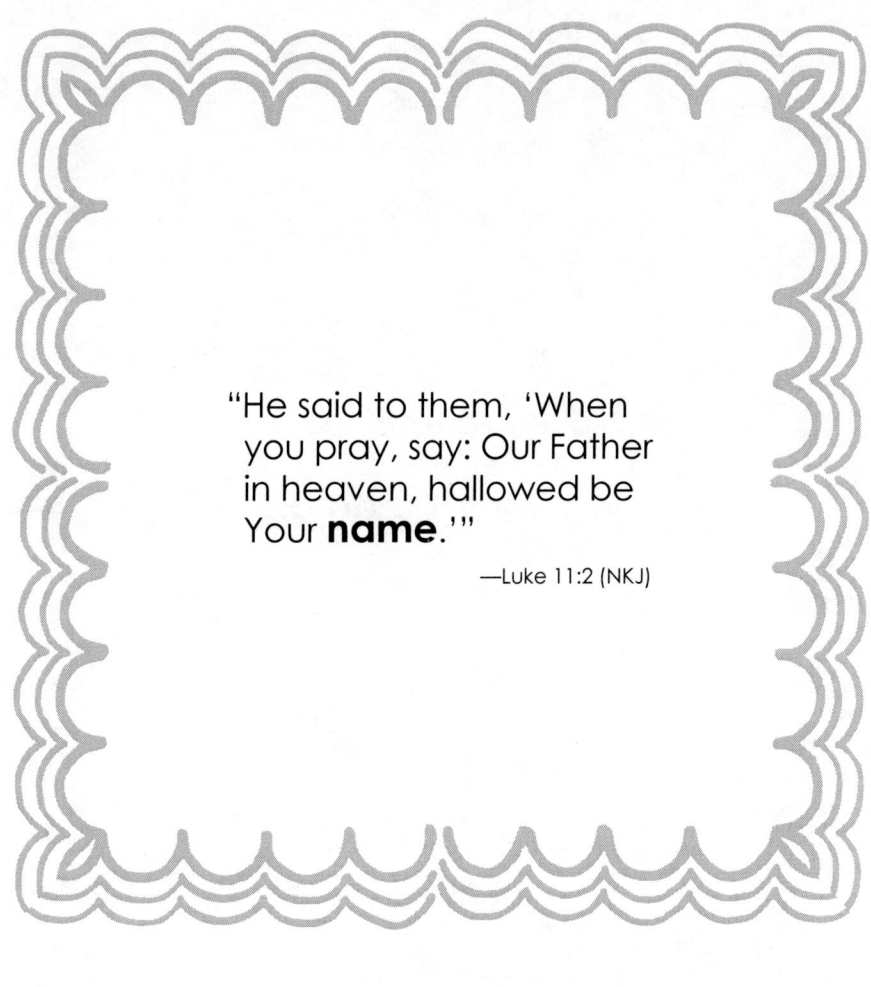

"He said to them, 'When you pray, say: Our Father in heaven, hallowed be Your **name**.'"

—Luke 11:2 (NKJ)

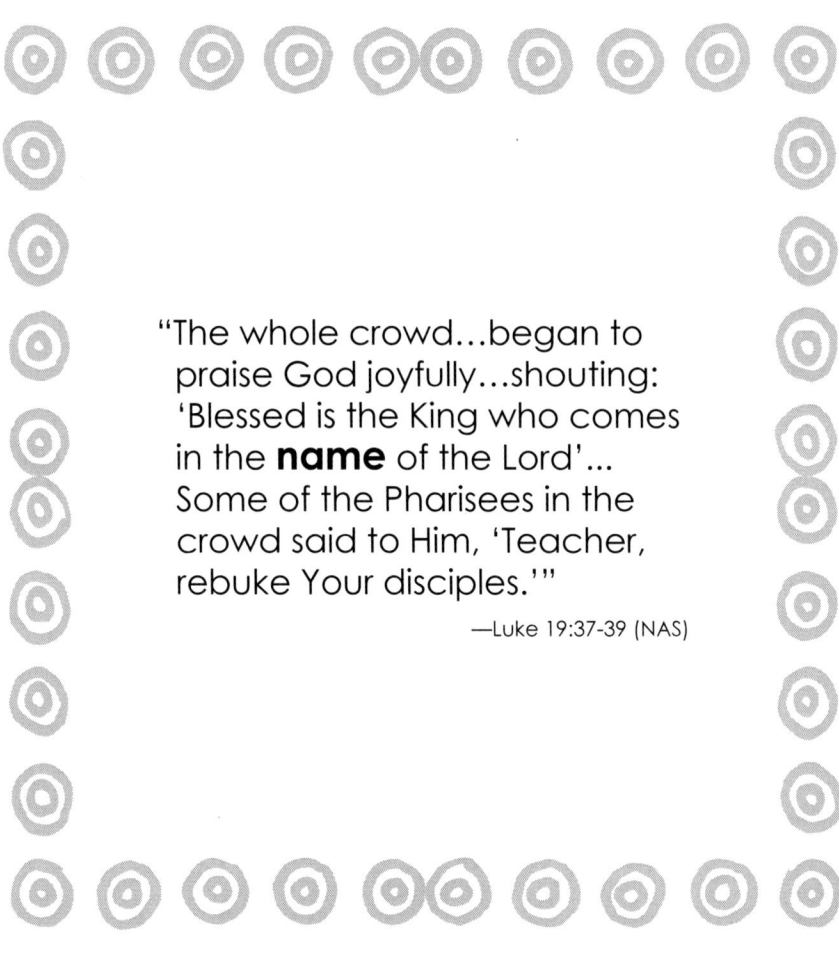

"The whole crowd…began to praise God joyfully…shouting: 'Blessed is the King who comes in the **name** of the Lord'… Some of the Pharisees in the crowd said to Him, 'Teacher, rebuke Your disciples.'"

—Luke 19:37-39 (NAS)

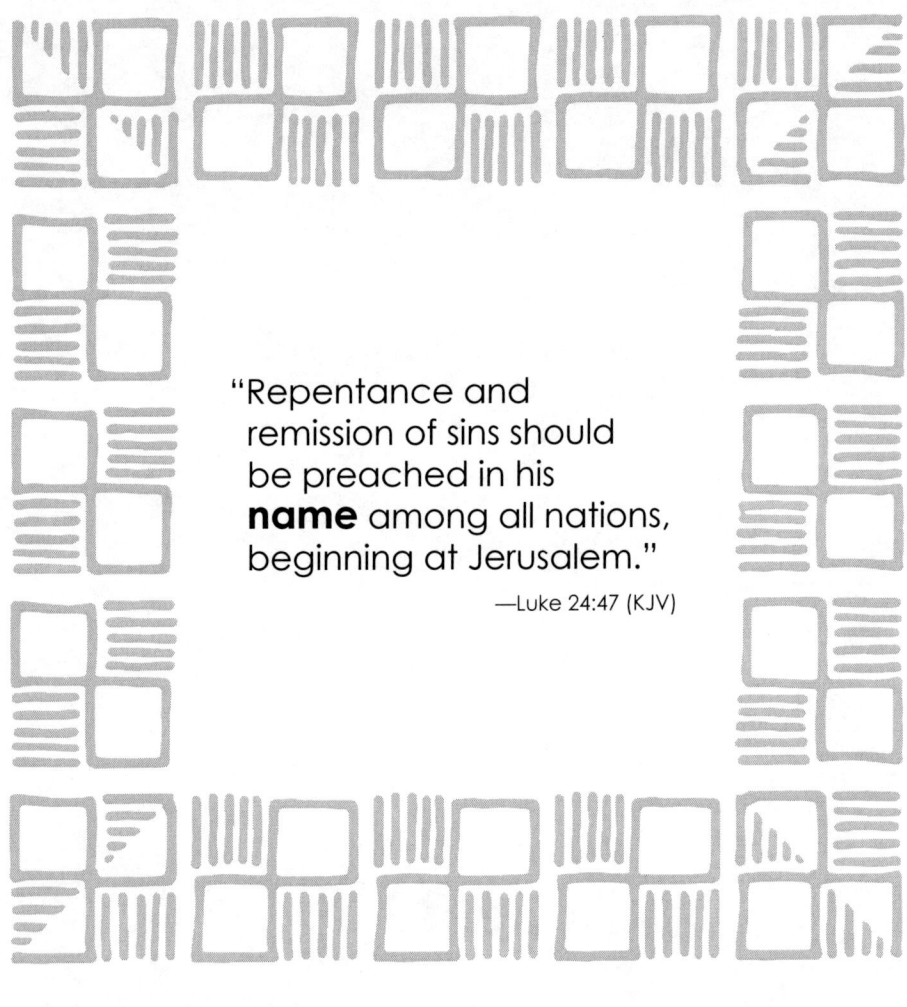

"Repentance and remission of sins should be preached in his **name** among all nations, beginning at Jerusalem."

—Luke 24:47 (KJV)

"To as many as did receive and welcome Him, He gave the right [the authority, the privilege] to become children of God, that is, to those who believe in (adhere to, trust in, and rely on) His **name**."

—John 1:12 (AMP)

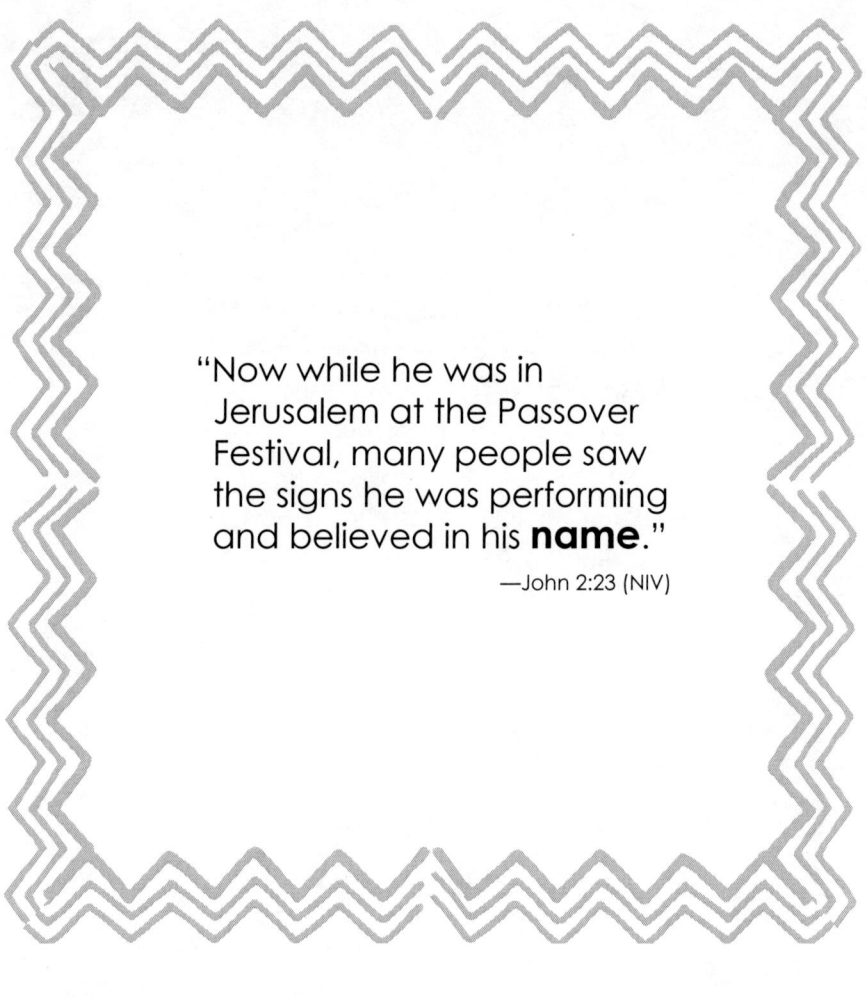

"Now while he was in Jerusalem at the Passover Festival, many people saw the signs he was performing and believed in his **name**."

—John 2:23 (NIV)

"Father, glorify thy **name**. Then came there a voice from heaven, saying, I have both glorified it, and will glorify it again."

—John 12:28 (KJV)

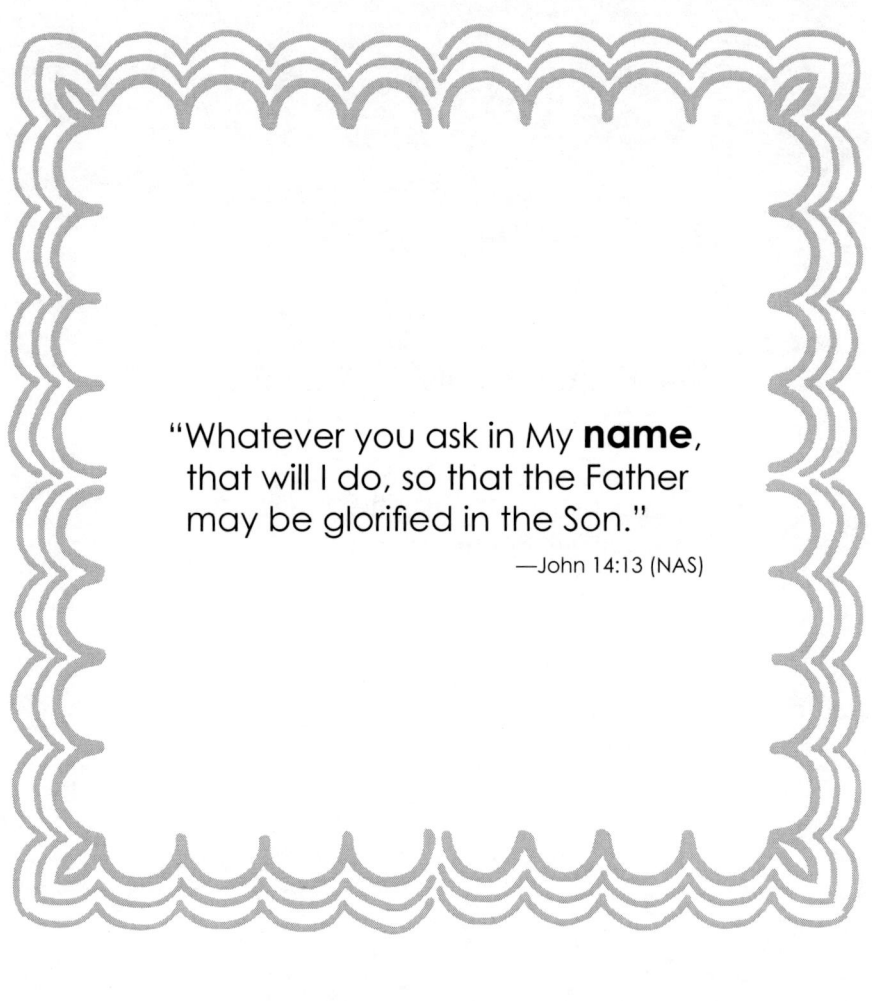

"Whatever you ask in My **name**, that will I do, so that the Father may be glorified in the Son."

—John 14:13 (NAS)

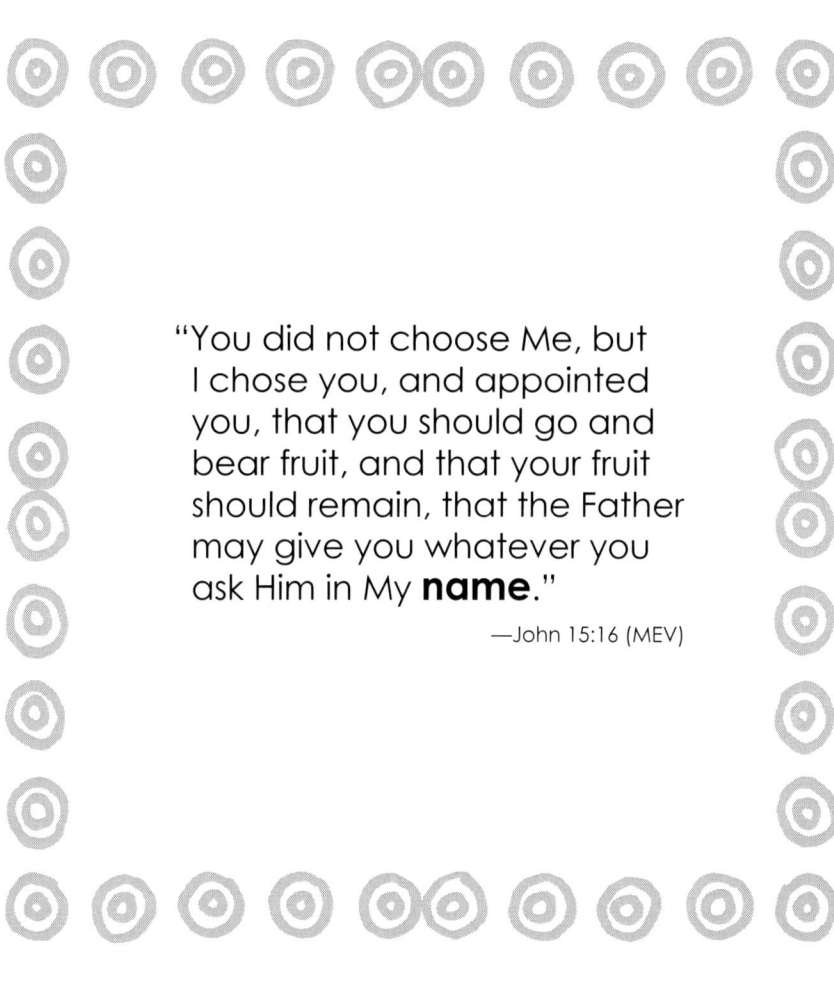

"You did not choose Me, but I chose you, and appointed you, that you should go and bear fruit, and that your fruit should remain, that the Father may give you whatever you ask Him in My **name**."

—John 15:16 (MEV)

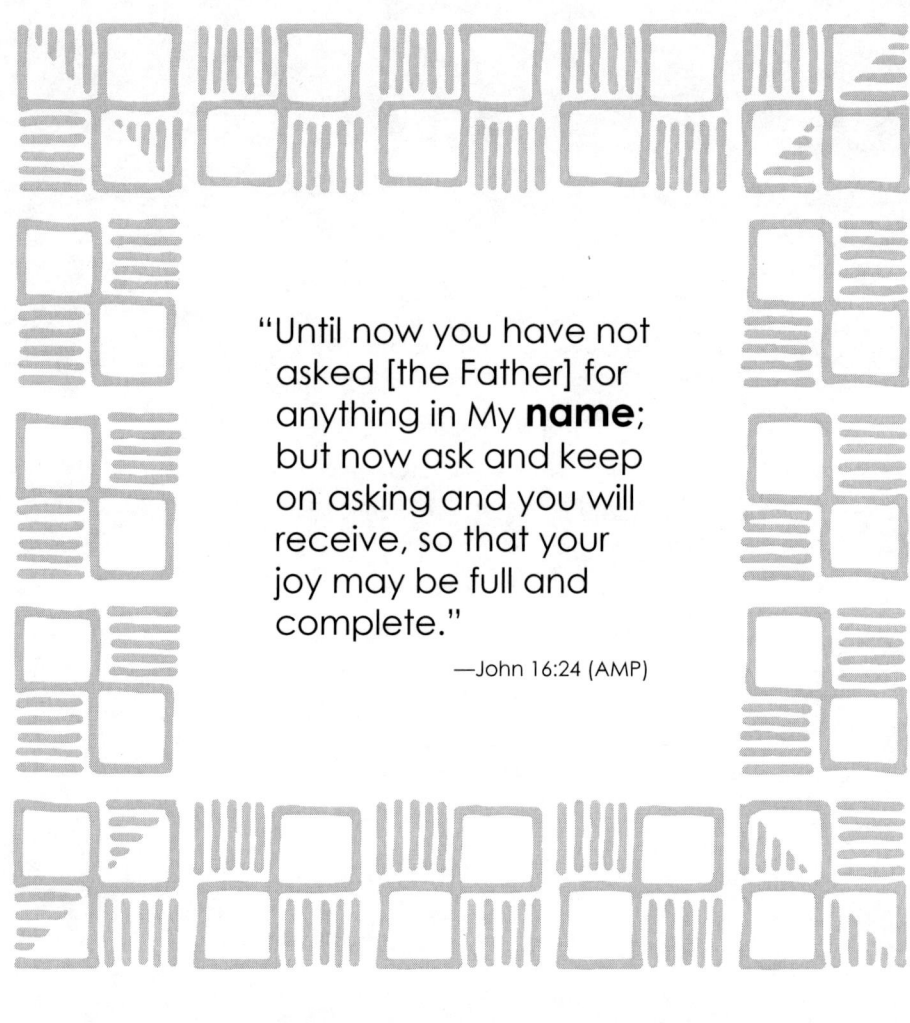

"Until now you have not asked [the Father] for anything in My **name**; but now ask and keep on asking and you will receive, so that your joy may be full and complete."

—John 16:24 (AMP)

"Holy Father, through Your **name** keep those whom You have given Me, that they may be one as We are one."

—John 17:11 (MEV)

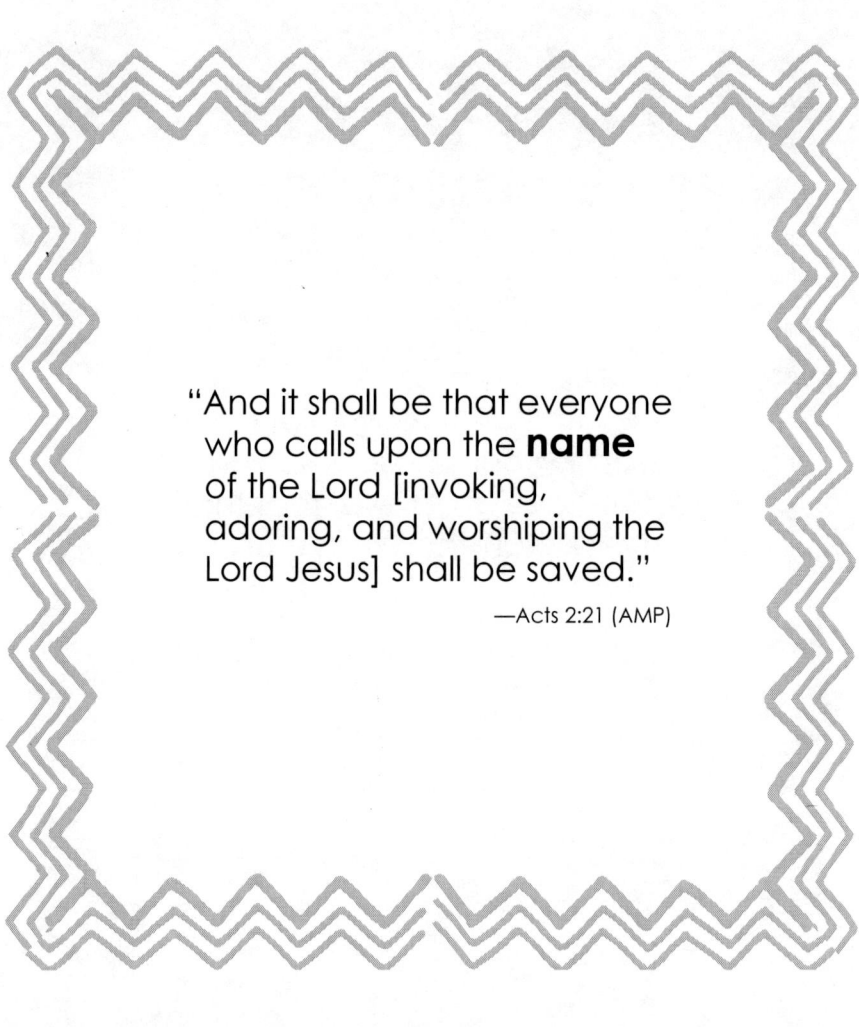

"And it shall be that everyone who calls upon the **name** of the Lord [invoking, adoring, and worshiping the Lord Jesus] shall be saved."

—Acts 2:21 (AMP)

"Repent [change your old way of thinking, turn from your sinful ways, accept and follow Jesus as the Messiah] and be baptized, each of you, in the **name** of Jesus Christ because of the forgiveness of your sins; and you will receive the gift of the Holy Spirit."

—Acts 2:38 (AMP)

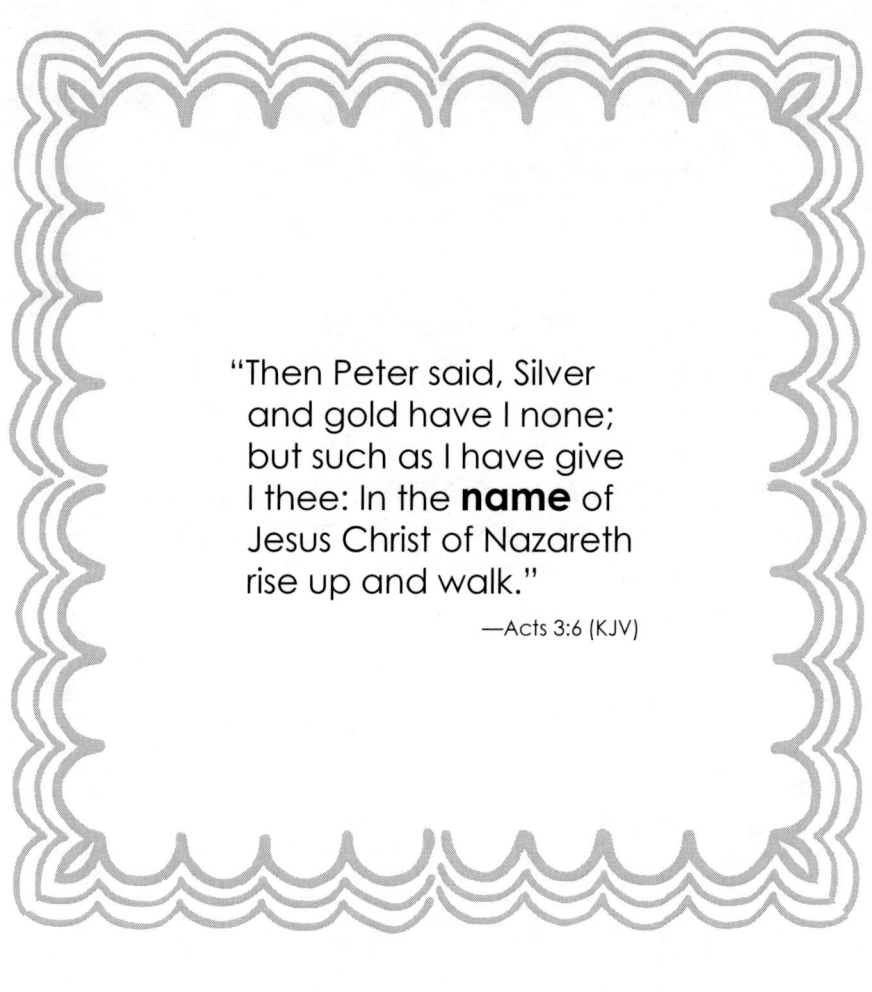

"Then Peter said, Silver and gold have I none; but such as I have give I thee: In the **name** of Jesus Christ of Nazareth rise up and walk."

—Acts 3:6 (KJV)

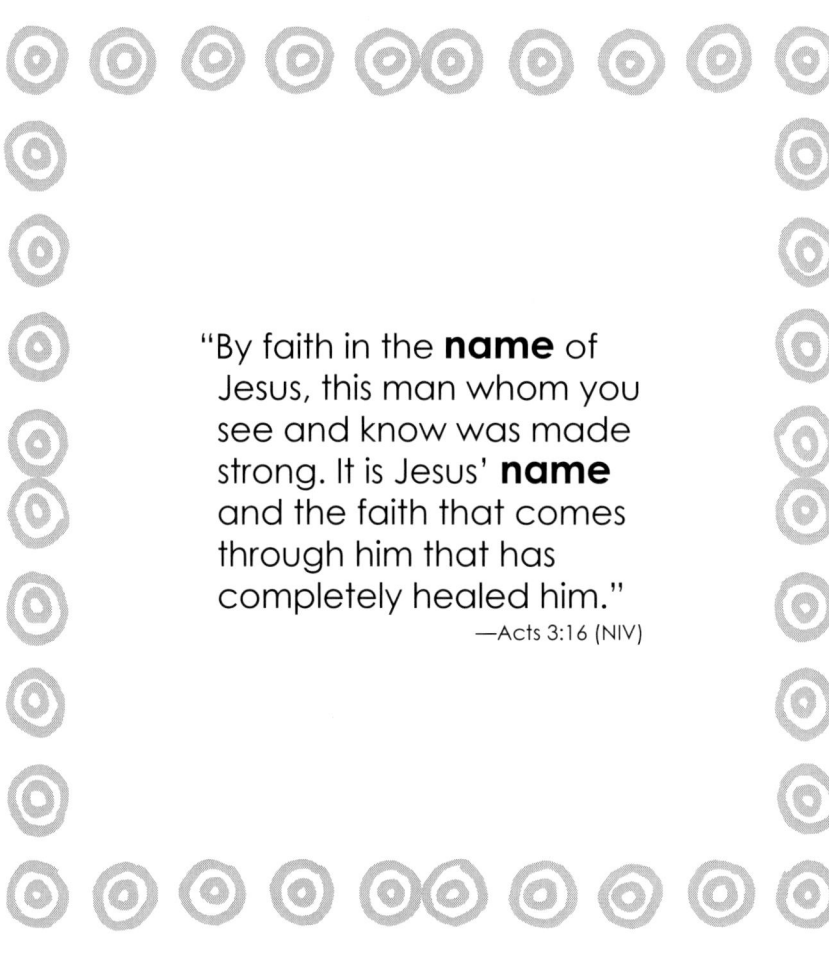

"By faith in the **name** of Jesus, this man whom you see and know was made strong. It is Jesus' **name** and the faith that comes through him that has completely healed him."

—Acts 3:16 (NIV)

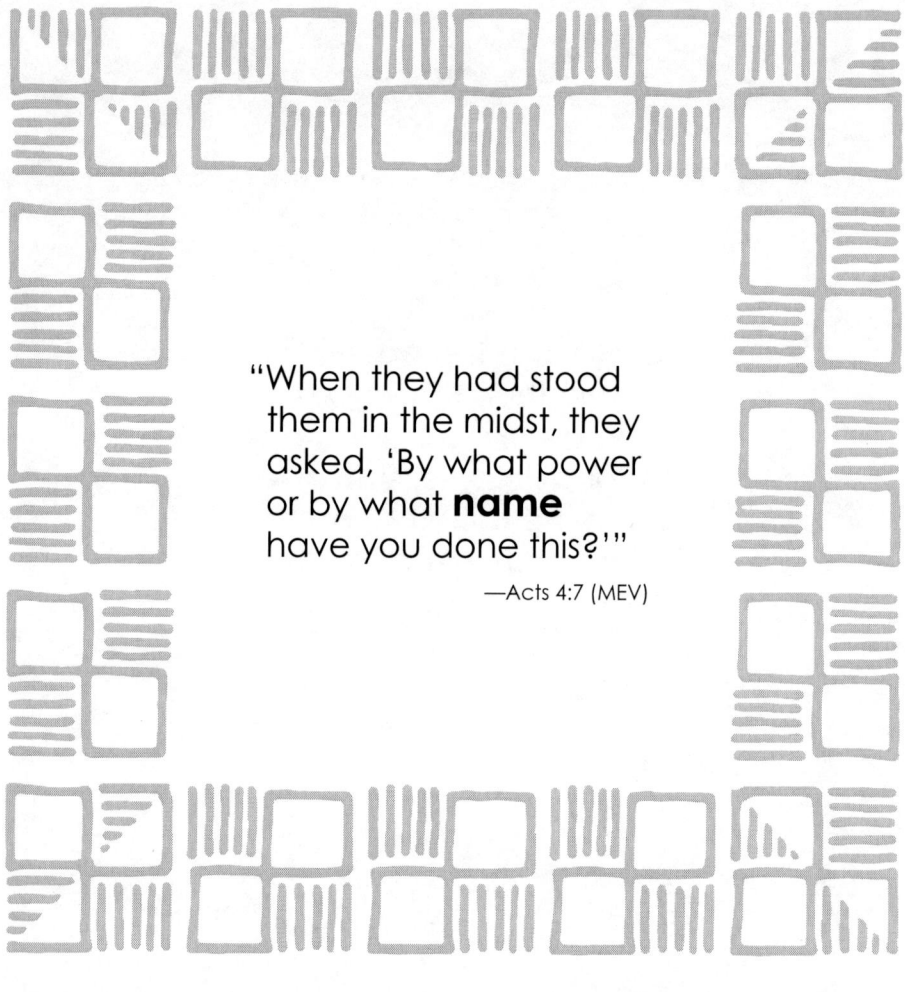

"When they had stood them in the midst, they asked, 'By what power or by what **name** have you done this?'"

—Acts 4:7 (MEV)

"Salvation is found in no one else, for there is no other **name** under heaven given to mankind by which we must be saved."

—Acts 4:12 (NIV)

"They…commanded them not to speak or teach at all in the **name** of Jesus. But Peter and John answered them, 'Whether it is right in the sight of God to listen to you more than to God, you judge. For we cannot help but declare what we have seen and heard.'"

—Acts 4:18-20 (MEV)

"Now, Lord, consider their threats and enable your servants to speak your word with great boldness. Stretch out your hand to heal and perform signs and wonders through the **name** of your holy servant Jesus."

—Acts 4:29-30 (NIV)

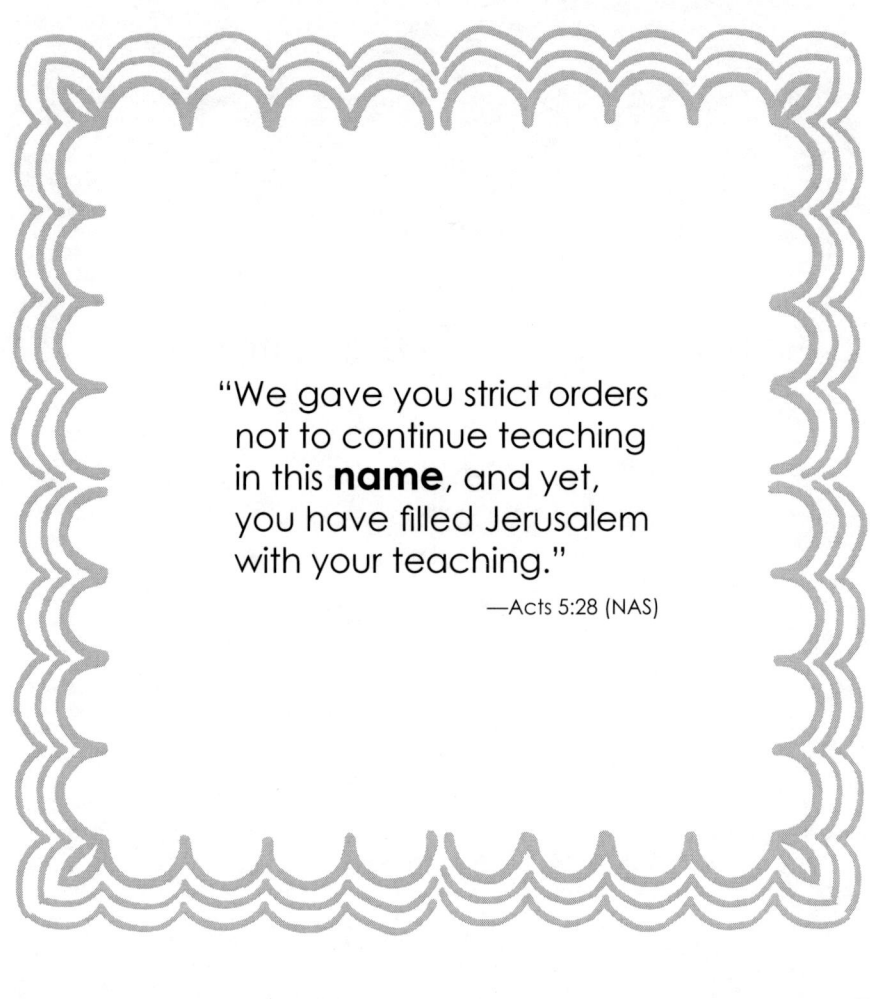

"We gave you strict orders not to continue teaching in this **name**, and yet, you have filled Jerusalem with your teaching."

—Acts 5:28 (NAS)

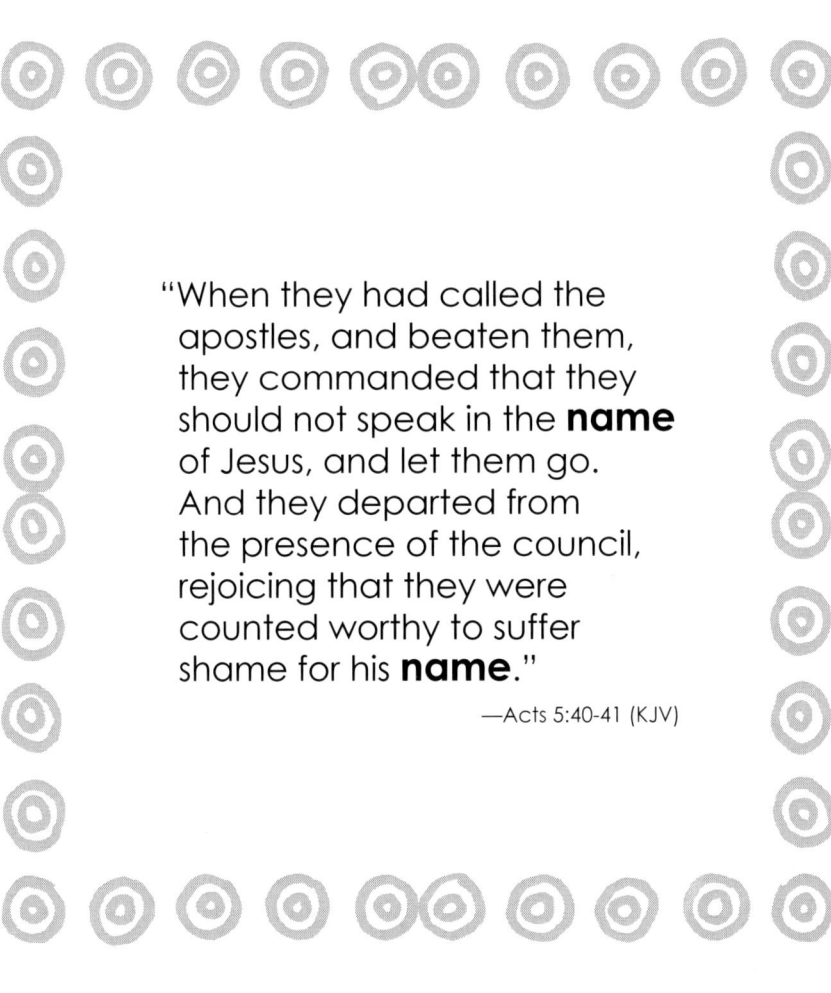

"When they had called the apostles, and beaten them, they commanded that they should not speak in the **name** of Jesus, and let them go. And they departed from the presence of the council, rejoicing that they were counted worthy to suffer shame for his **name**."

—Acts 5:40-41 (KJV)

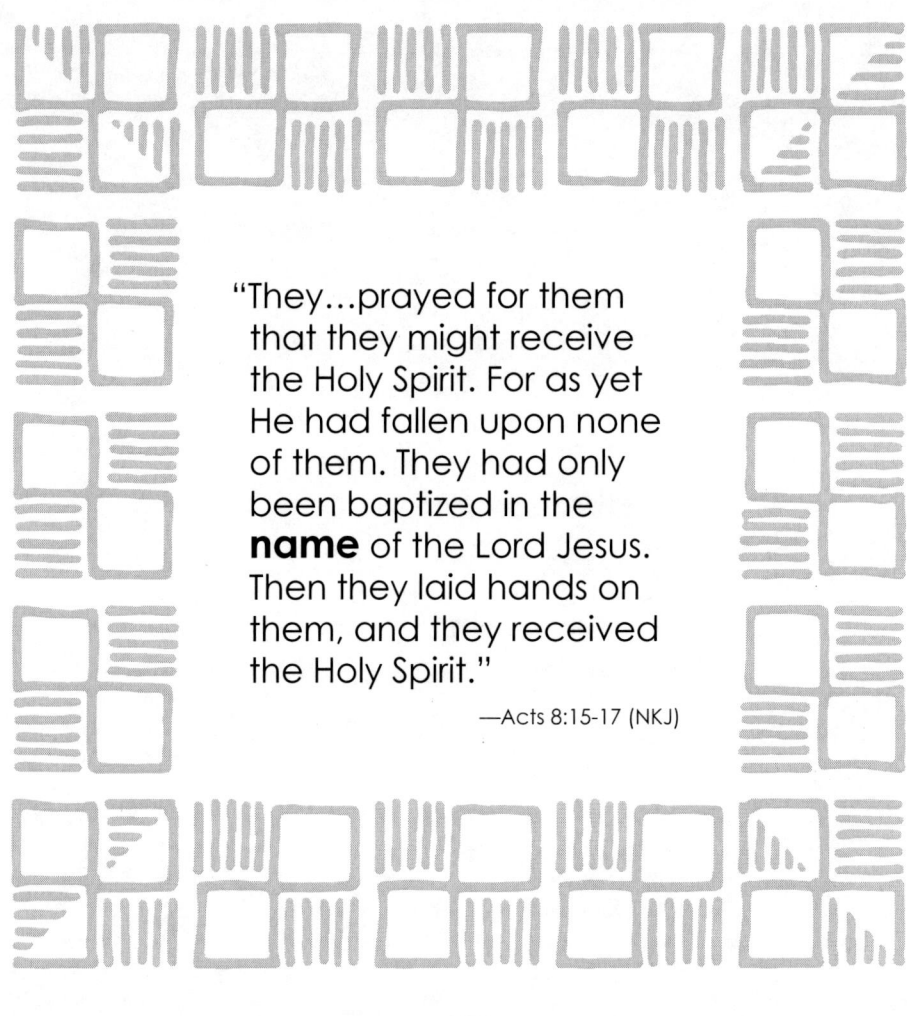

"They...prayed for them that they might receive the Holy Spirit. For as yet He had fallen upon none of them. They had only been baptized in the **name** of the Lord Jesus. Then they laid hands on them, and they received the Holy Spirit."

—Acts 8:15-17 (NKJ)

"And he spoke boldly in the **name** of the Lord Jesus…but they attempted to kill him."

—Acts 9:29 (NKJ)

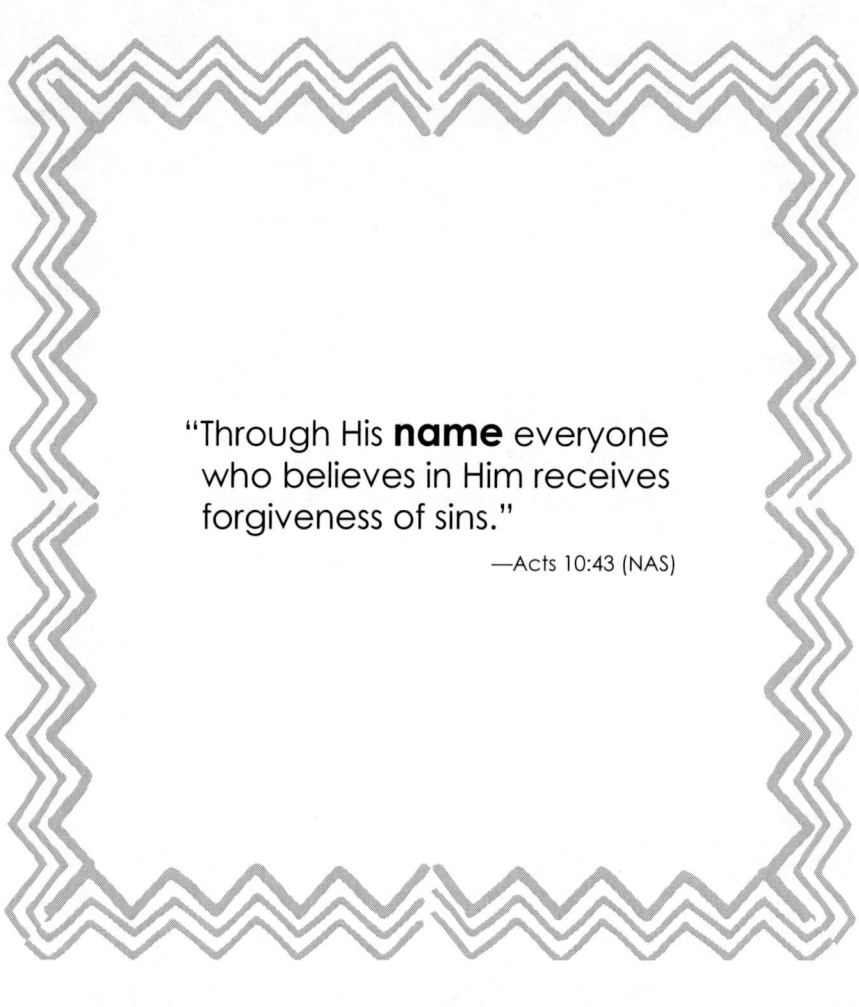

"Through His **name** everyone who believes in Him receives forgiveness of sins."

—Acts 10:43 (NAS)

"Paul, greatly annoyed, turned and said to the spirit, 'I command you in the **name** of Jesus Christ to come out of her.' And he came out that very hour."

—Acts 16:18 (NKJ)

"When they heard this, they were baptized in the **name** of the Lord Jesus."

—Acts 19:5 (KJV)

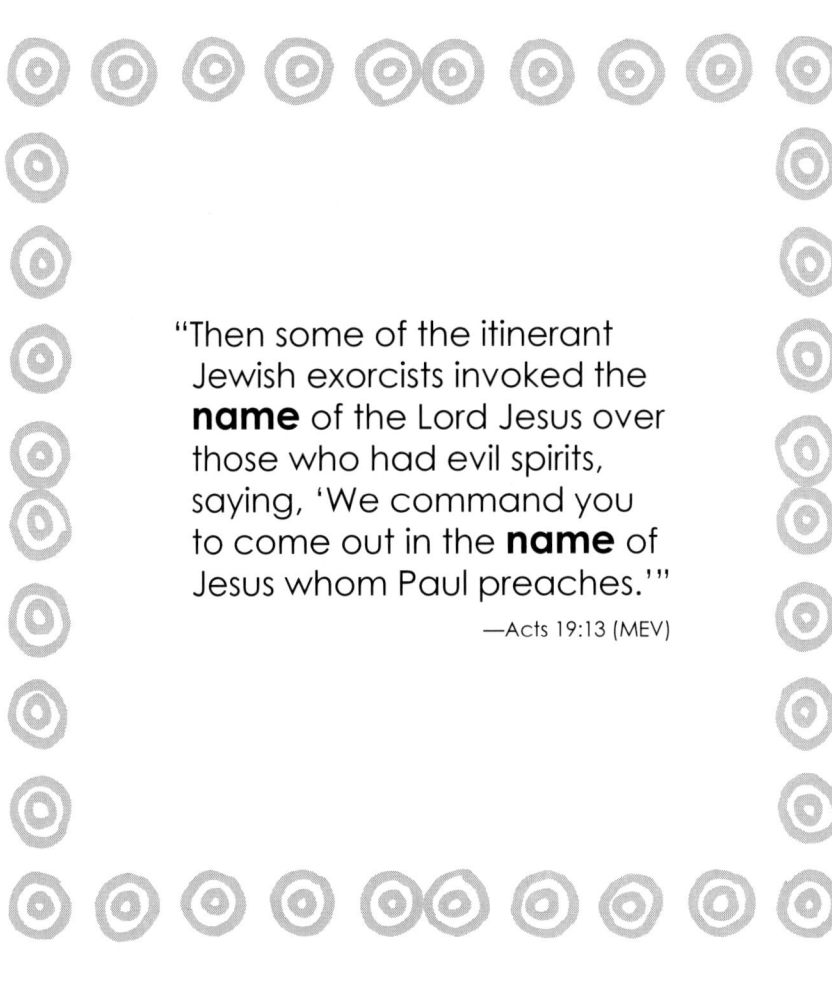

"Then some of the itinerant Jewish exorcists invoked the **name** of the Lord Jesus over those who had evil spirits, saying, 'We command you to come out in the **name** of Jesus whom Paul preaches.'"

—Acts 19:13 (MEV)

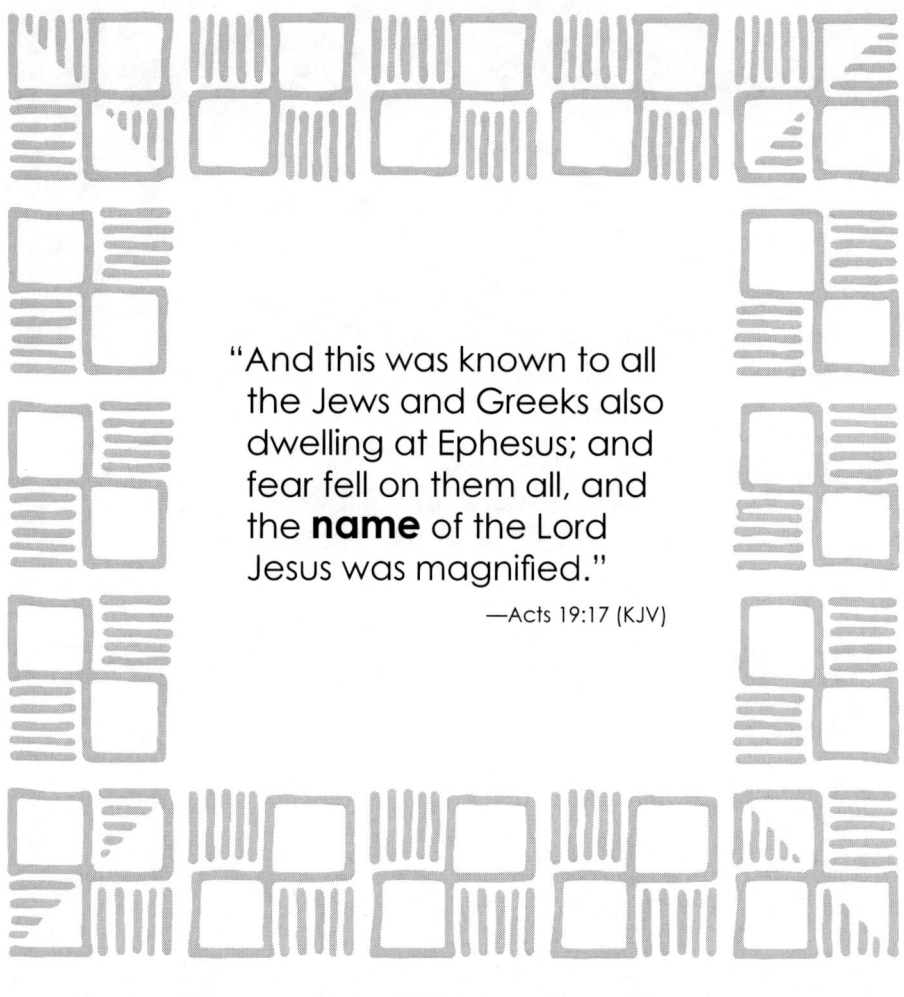

"And this was known to all the Jews and Greeks also dwelling at Ephesus; and fear fell on them all, and the **name** of the Lord Jesus was magnified."

—Acts 19:17 (KJV)

"Then Paul answered, 'What are you doing, weeping and breaking my heart? For I am ready not only to be bound, but even to die at Jerusalem for the **name** of the Lord Jesus.'"

—Acts 21:13 (NAS)

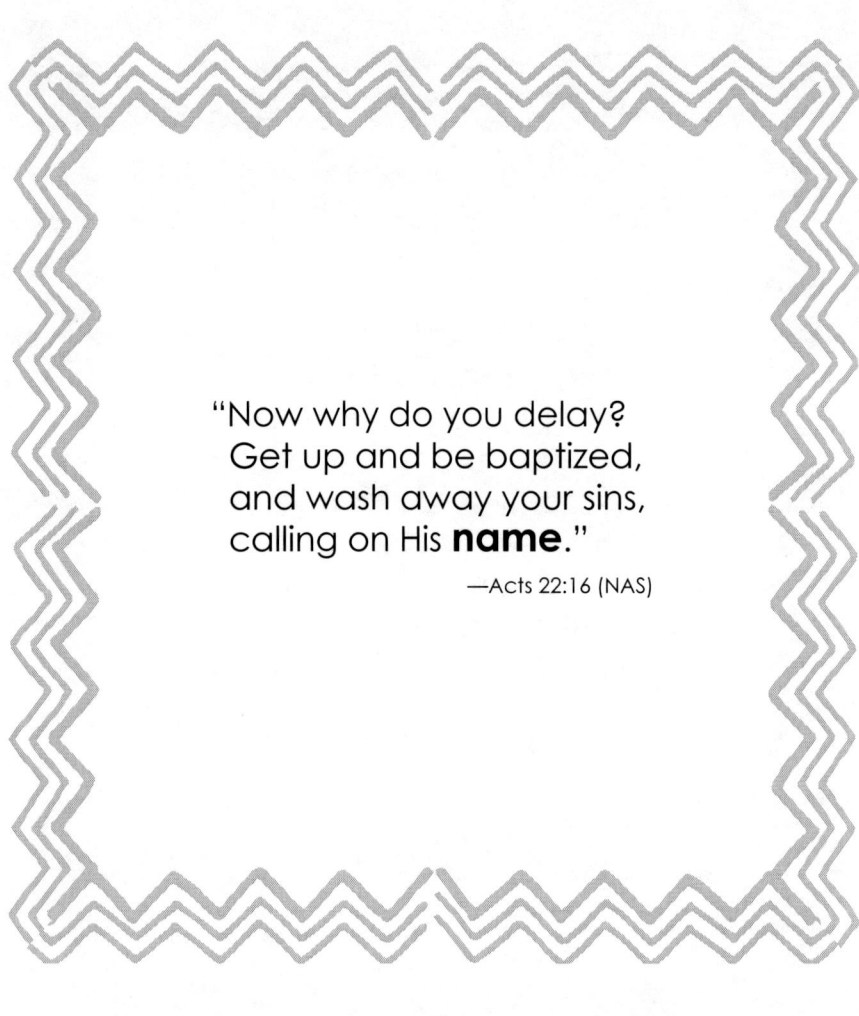

"Now why do you delay? Get up and be baptized, and wash away your sins, calling on His **name**."

—Acts 22:16 (NAS)

"For whosoever shall call upon the **name** of the Lord shall be saved."

—Romans 10:13 (KJV)

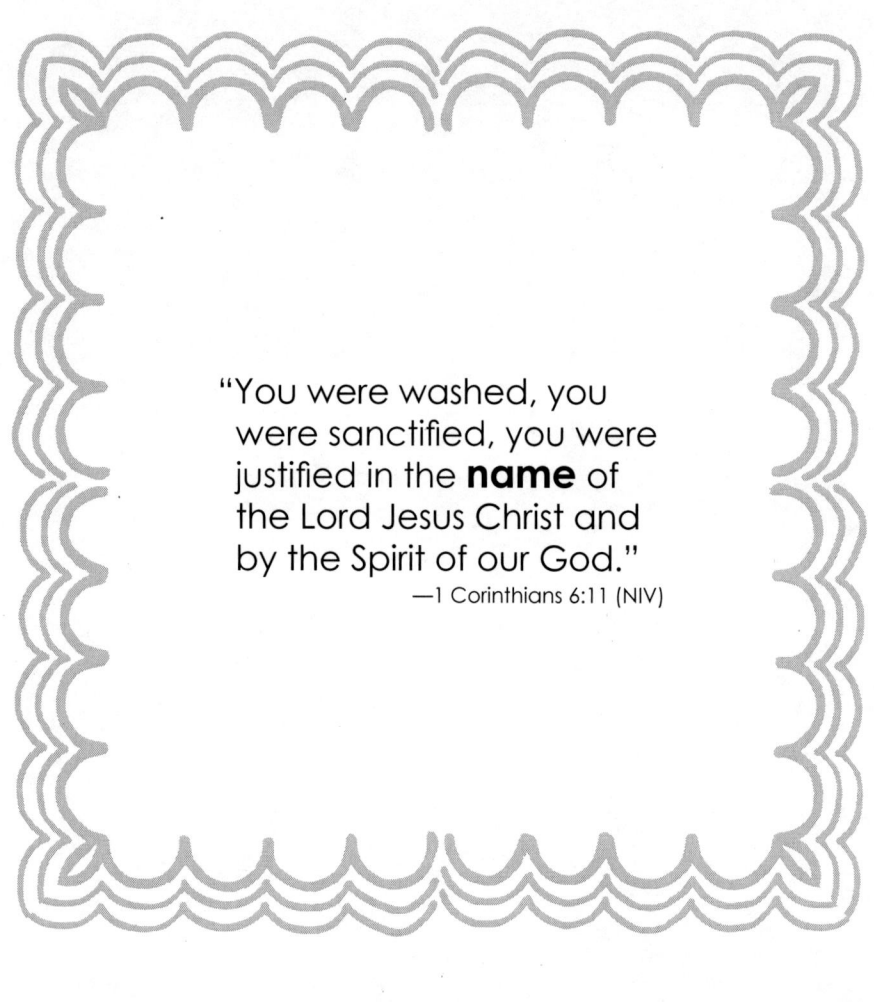

"You were washed, you were sanctified, you were justified in the **name** of the Lord Jesus Christ and by the Spirit of our God."
—1 Corinthians 6:11 (NIV)

"For this reason I bow my knees before the Father, from whom every family in heaven and on earth derives its **name**."

—Ephesians 3:14-15 (NAS)

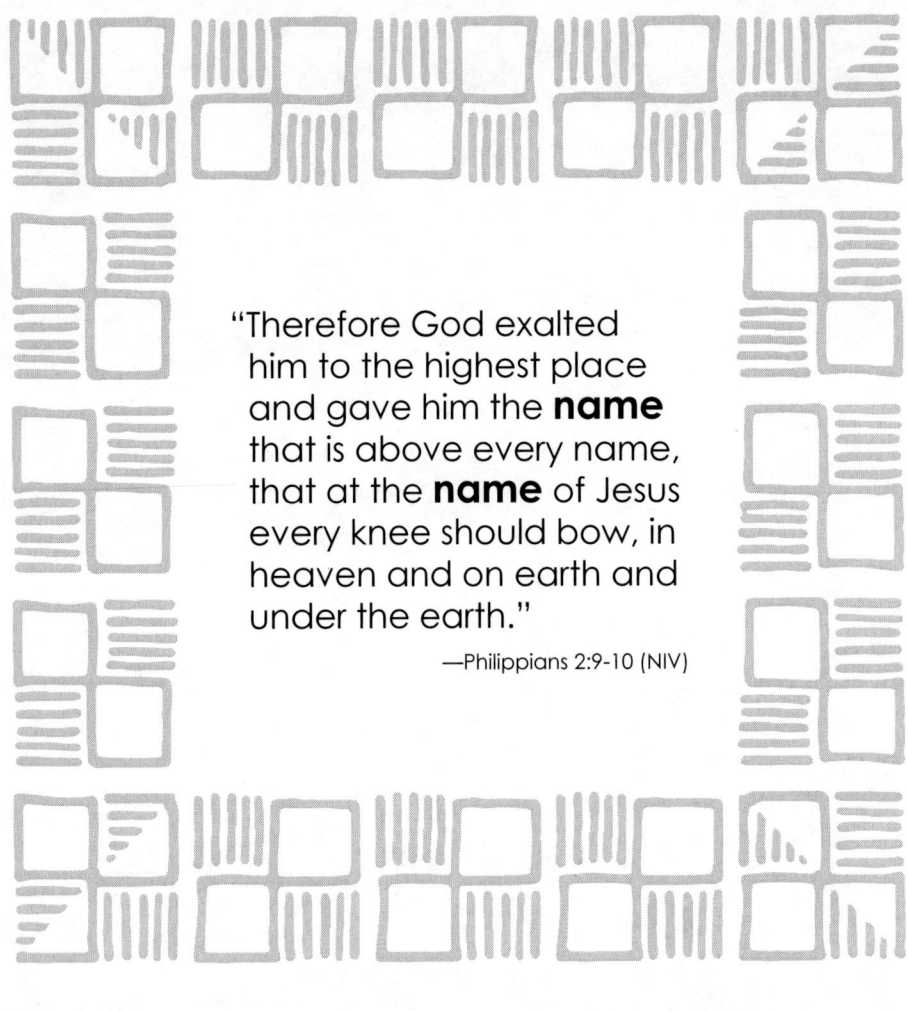

"Therefore God exalted him to the highest place and gave him the **name** that is above every name, that at the **name** of Jesus every knee should bow, in heaven and on earth and under the earth."

—Philippians 2:9-10 (NIV)

"Whatever you do in word or deed, do all in the **name** of the Lord Jesus, giving thanks through Him to God the Father."

—Colossians 3:17 (NAS)

"To this end also we pray for you always, that our God will count you worthy of your calling, and fulfill every desire for goodness and the work of faith with power, so that the **name** of our Lord Jesus will be glorified in you."

—2 Thessalonians 1:11-12 (NAS)

"Is any sick among you? Let him call for the elders of the church; and let them pray over him, anointing him with oil in the **name** of the Lord."

—James 5:14 (KJV)

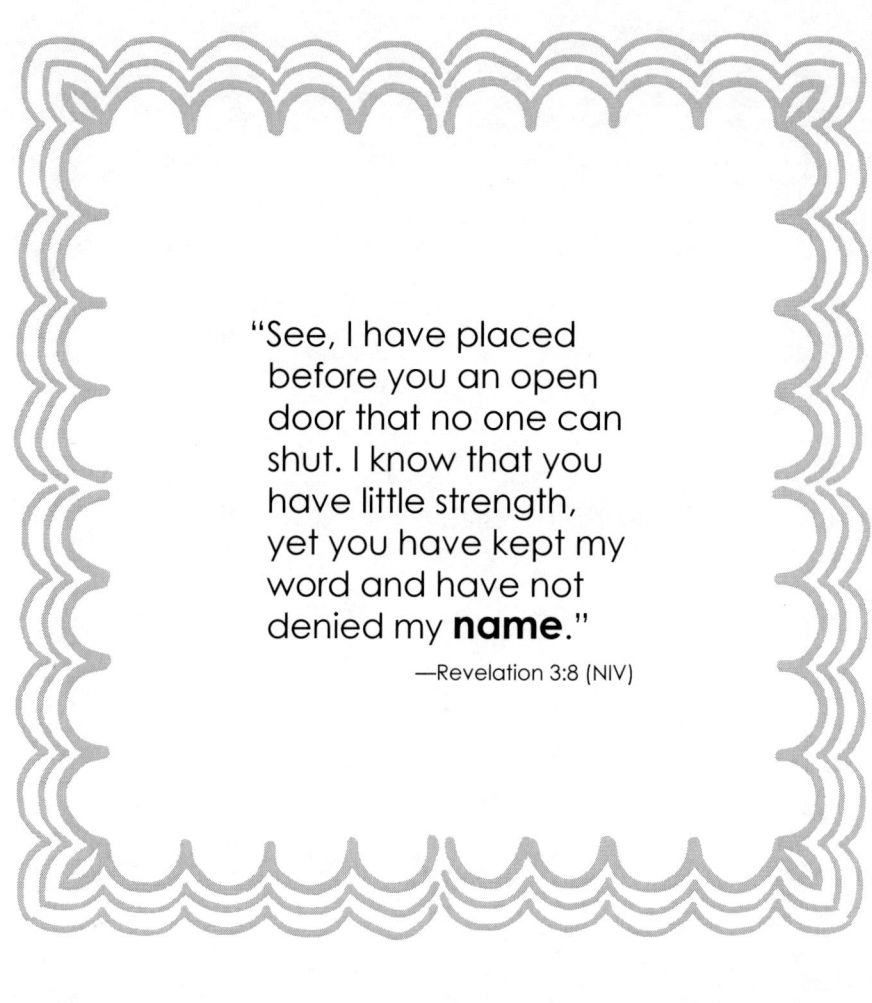

"See, I have placed before you an open door that no one can shut. I know that you have little strength, yet you have kept my word and have not denied my **name**."

—Revelation 3:8 (NIV)

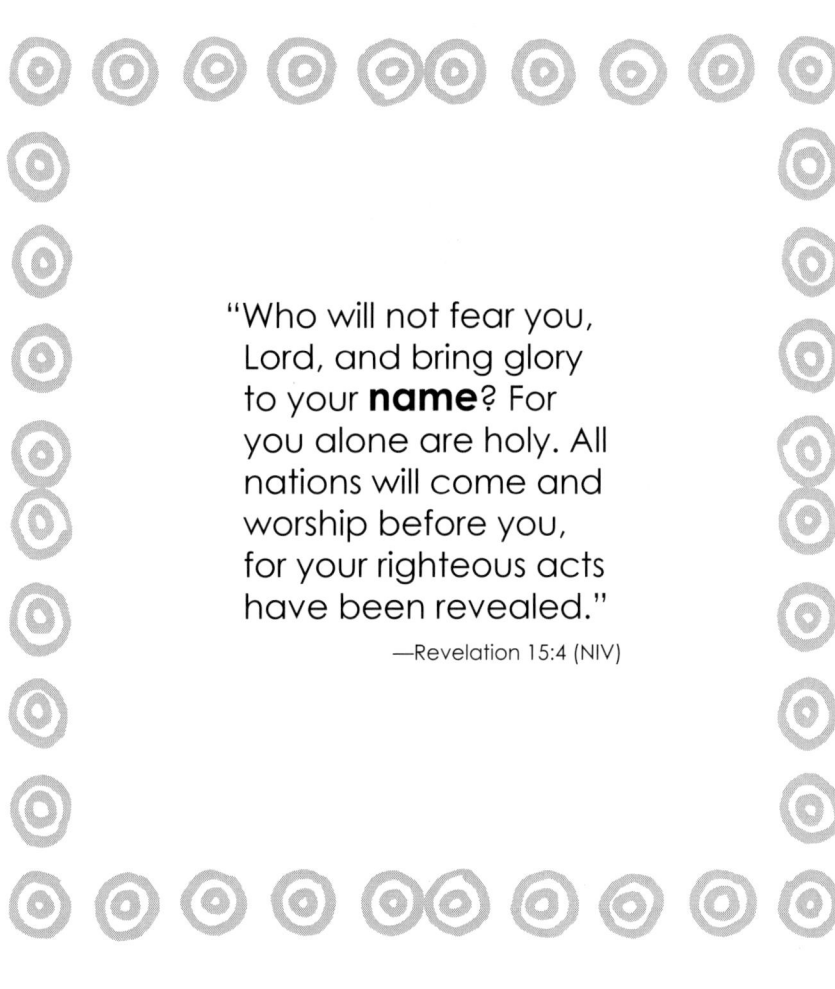

"Who will not fear you, Lord, and bring glory to your **name**? For you alone are holy. All nations will come and worship before you, for your righteous acts have been revealed."

—Revelation 15:4 (NIV)

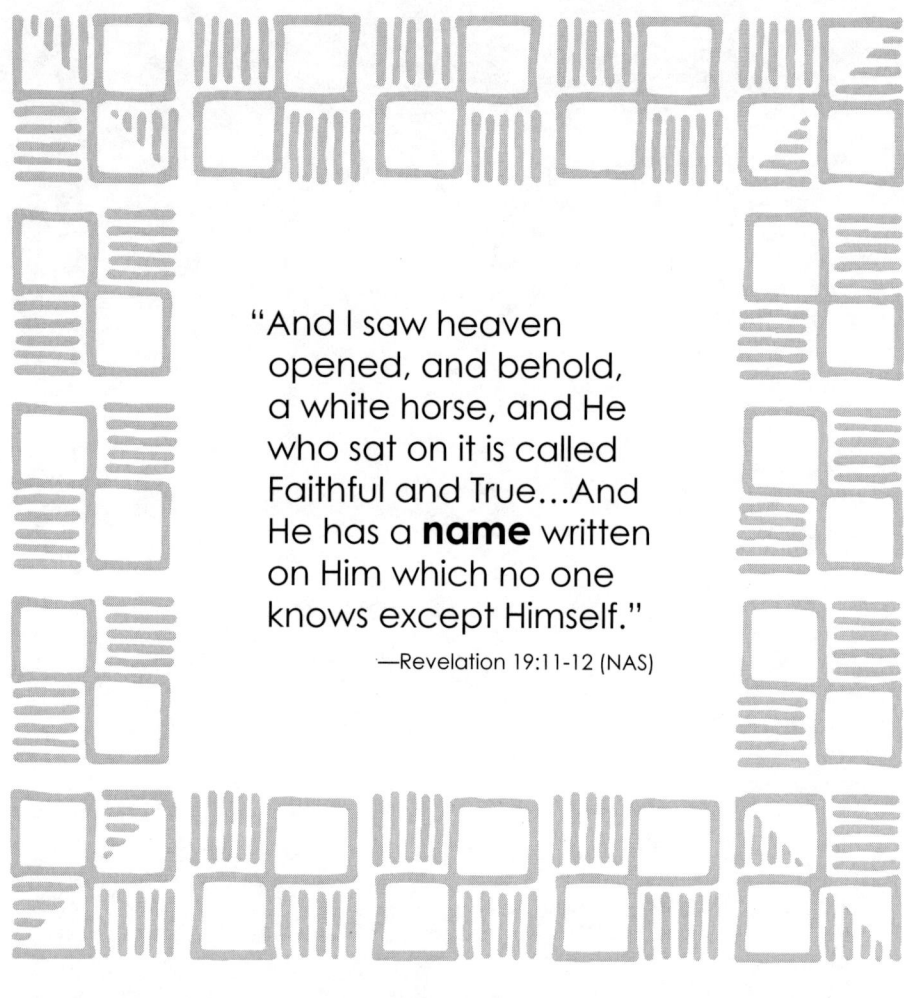

"And I saw heaven opened, and behold, a white horse, and He who sat on it is called Faithful and True…And He has a **name** written on Him which no one knows except Himself."

—Revelation 19:11-12 (NAS)

"There will no longer be any curse; and the throne of God and of the Lamb will be in it, and His bond-servants will serve Him; they will see His face, and His **name** will be on their foreheads."

—Revelation 22:3-4 (NAS)

Notes

Notes

Notes

Books by Diana Scimone

"Proclaiming God's Word" series:
- The Justice Book
- The Love Book
- The Mercy Book
- The Kingdom Book
- The Truth Book
- The Titles of God Book
- The Name of God Book
- The Righteousness Book
- The Healing Book
- The Wisdom Book
- The Destiny Book
- and more

To subscribe, see www.peapodpublishing.com.

Audacious
Who Wants My Cheese?
Adventures With PawPaw: China
Adventures With PawPaw: France
Adventures With PawPaw: Costa Rica
Born to Fly

A portion of all book sales benefits the Born2Fly Project to stop child trafficking (www.born2fly.org).

Contact

Peapod Publishing Inc.
PO Box 951599
Lake Mary, Florida 32795 U.S.A.

info@peapodpublishing.com
www.peapodpublishing.com
Twitter: @DianaScimone
Facebook: Peapod Publishing

Diana Scimone is a former journalist who has traveled to more than 40 countries writing about justice and human rights including Sudan, Zimbabwe, and China. She is president of the Born2Fly Project to stop child trafficking and is author of numerous books for adults and children.

Made in United States
Cleveland, OH
02 December 2025